How Senior Marketers Scale the Heights

WHAT IS STILL TRUE, MORE TRUE & NEWLY TRUE

By Nancie McDonnell Ruder

Keep scaling the heights!

N— McD—ll R—

ISBN: 978-1-66786-619-2

Edited by Alyson Gold Weinberg and Emily Schultz
Cover, book design and illustrations by Jenn Spencer
Cover photo by Lexi Moore Photography

To my children: Sydney, Stephen and Samantha

"When someone else's happiness
is your happiness, that is love."

Lana del Rey

TABLE OF CONTENTS

FORWARD

By Ann Mukherjee
(former) Global Chief Marketing Officer, SC Johnson
(now) Chairman and CEO, Pernod Ricard NA

AOL, Kodak, Polaroid, Enron, Lehman Brothers, Circuit City, Toys "R" Us, DHL, Borders, Blockbuster... Change is the only constant today. Doing the same thing over and over again and expecting a different outcome isn't just insanity; it could mean extinction. Twenty-five years ago, when I became a marketer, the function was very clearly defined. Our jobs were to create loyalty and value for products and services through brand building so the companies we worked for could profitably sell the supply they efficiently made. We were in charge: we controlled the information and content consumers and shoppers received, controlled the channels in which they purchased our brands and controlled the prices they paid. And then technology democratized the world, creating a new normal. Consumers and shoppers now have Star-Trek-like devices in their hands and they are in control. Today they have infinite choices of not only what to buy, but when, how and at what price. Rule books for marketing went out the window. The tables turned. Our jobs were no longer about how to market what our companies could efficiently supply; instead, we became change agents, helping our companies evolve so they could profitably supply what consumers now demanded.

For entrepreneurially-minded marketers, this was nirvana. Barriers to entry that companies had built over decades were now crashing down and with liberated consumers demanding more for their money, new companies and services were being born by the hour. To survive, we as marketers needed to evolve; we needed our own renaissance. Like da Vinci, we needed to extract the art from the science, and in turn, make the art drive predictable value. As competition and change are now driven by the very consumers we need to win over, we must balance science and art to make the unpredictable predictable.

I learned this the hard way: through failure. I have come to realize that failure has been the S curve of my personal growth, each failure unlocking new capabilities and unleashing new potential in my abilities. During my first major life failure, I met Nancie. We were both MBA students at the University of Chicago's Booth School of Business. As an Asian Indian, I was brought up to respect science (culturally, you were only successful as an engineer or doctor... my family was littered with both). For every problem, I felt there had to be one perfect answer, derived scientifically, mathematically and logically. The fact there could be multiple answers eluded me—I wasn't comfortable with ambiguity and uncertainty. Nancie, who is a born coach, adopted me as I struggled through my classes and approach to learning. Nancie has a unique ability to analyze and synthesize behavior, helping people bridge gaps to see possibilities. She pushed my thinking and helped me believe in my common sense, my judgement and my gut to bring together logic and creativity, inventing solutions rather than just solving problems.

Over the years and throughout my career, Nancie has played a pivotal role in helping me to live my ambition of Transforming

Tomorrow Today. When Nancie formally founded Noetic Consultants, she worked with my teams and myself to create change agendas. In my quest to create learning organizations, Nancie has been pivotal in creating new ways to master and operationalize today's brand of disruptive marketing. She has combined her years of experience with Leo Burnett with her natural coaching capabilities to create unique approaches to systemize left and right brain ways of working. Creating substantive organizational change is never easy, but her practical approach helped me land transformation in ways that created high-performance teams that know how to battle in this new Volatile, Uncertain, Complex and Ambiguous (VUCA) world we compete in. She has taken this same practical approach in this book. If you are a marketer, or anyone tasked with creating growth for your company, this is a fantastic guidebook. It will help you feel more empowered, perceive your own possibilities and see where you need to stretch, while giving you practical, actionable steps on how best to succeed. If your ambition is to aim high, you need to master not only what you do but how to do it, the right mind set and that last 10% that makes the difference between good and truly great. This book will definitely show you how.

CHAPTER ONE

Pass the Secret Sauce

If you picked up this book, you've probably been working in the marketing field for a while. I bet you're ambitious, at least somewhat, if not very, established in your career and ready to take it to the next level. Perhaps you recognize the shifting media and technological landscape and want to get ahead of the next curve, or at least feel more adept at keeping up with the breakneck speed of change. Maybe, like so many of us in the ranks of senior marketers, you're feeling a little like an "old dog" who could use some new tricks. Don't take this the wrong way; those of us who know that we don't know everything are already ahead of the game. And what exactly is an old dog, anyway? As Henry Ford says, "Anyone who stops learning is old, whether at twenty or eighty. Anyone who keeps learning stays young." So, really, we're all just pups.

No matter what brought you to these pages, you were likely intrigued by the potential to glean insights from your most successful peers and that quality, your curiosity, is a large part of what got you this far, so keep reading. Fellow senior marketers are our best teachers. In more than 25+ years as a marketer, I've seen how much the most thriving and striving among us can teach. I have had the honor of working in and with large and small domestic and international companies, supporting senior marketers in their most complex business challenges.

I have experienced their struggles and triumphs and gained a lot from both. Working with these individuals and companies—first as an in-house marketer at Leo Burnett and later in my work as principal of my own consultancy, Noetic—I began to see patterns emerge. There were similarities in the challenges my most successful coworkers, colleagues and clients faced and the means by which they were able to navigate them. There were traits that stood out among those whose work I admired most. They embodied surprising and sometimes seemingly paradoxical qualities. As I observed these commonalities among the most agile and adept of us, I saw a theory of success coalesce. This book is a distillation of that theory.

To paraphrase the iconic Leo Burnett campaign, modern marketing is not your father's Oldsmobile. In order to drive products, services and careers where they need to go, today's senior marketers may need to hone some skills and trade in others for a newer model. It is my firm belief that the secrets to marketing success can, indeed, be taught and learned. There is a reason some excel and rise in our profession, even as the market shifts and changes, even as technology moves at an ever-accelerating pace. Inspired by those who have reached the apex of the field and as a marketer who loves evidence that grounds stories as much as the storytelling itself, I knew I had to confirm what I was coming to believe was the senior marketer's "secret sauce."

So, I conducted more than 50 in-depth interviews of senior marketers, covering 20 different industries. I talked to men and women leading the way across the country and across the industry—senior marketers from ad agencies, art galleries, beer companies, sports conglomerates, media corporations, non-profit organizations and every other conceivable arena. In gathering and examining their collective experience and wisdom, I saw that while each senior marketer and his or her career trajectory is unique, they hold certain attributes and habits in common. These men and women are curious, culture-aware, keep current and continually learn. They are resilient, passionate and unafraid to take risks and fail. They have grit. Many seem to be Jacks- or Jills-of-all-trades, turning the phrase on its ear to transform "master of none" into "masters of marketing." And almost none of them chose the marketing path; the path seemed to choose them.

Through these discussions, I found another intriguing quality I believe is key to their success and it's what compelled me to write this book. Once these folks started to climb within their organization or field, it was the ability to apply what I call the "art" and "science" of their marketing discipline and know when to shift from one to the other, that got them to the top and kept them there.

According to John Maeda, author of *The Laws of Simplicity and Redesigning Leadership*, "Artists and scientists tend to approach problems with a similar open-mindedness and inquisitiveness— they both do not fear the unknown, preferring leaps to incremental steps. They make natural partners."

It stands to reason that those who harness the combined power of art and science within themselves and their careers and fields, expressing a facility with both sides and combining them for maximum effect, are especially potent. "There is real value to be gained from collaborations that bridge the best talents we have in both the quantitative and qualitative domains," says Maeda.

noetic *note*

When I founded my company, Noetic, more than 15 years ago, I was searching for a simple name that would also capture a sense of our unique approach to client work. I came upon the word "noetic," which means "thoughtful" or "wise." Since so much of what our team does is help clients think through difficult challenges that they didn't have the bandwidth or skillset to do on their own, this name felt exactly on-brand.

As I have gained a deeper understanding of the intersection of art and science in marketing work, I appreciate our name all the more. It's a true fusion of art and science. First and not insignificantly, it rhymes with "poetic," which helps folks remember the pronunciation.

Poetry, like all art, is a product of creativity, courtesy of the muse. And marketing without the muse is just flat. Of course, the muse alone isn't enough for great marketing—we also need data to proceed—so it's appropriate that we share the word noetic with the noetic sciences: the study of the metacognition of the brain, or how we think about thinking.

In these pages, we will hear straight from the marketers' mouths about how they developed their inherent gifts as well as how they developed workarounds for their weaknesses. We will explore the ways in which they use their expertise in both art and science to grow into respected leaders. We will understand how they pulled together strong teams made up of members who complement one another. We will learn the critical role mentors have played in their careers. And we will spell out, in concrete terms, how we can emulate the tools, tricks and strategies these outstanding members of our marketing tribe use to make art and science work for them.

I had a wonderful time researching and conducting the interviews for this book. I am deeply grateful that some of the busiest and most impressive marketers I know took the time to sit down and discuss their experiences with me so that I, in turn, could share them with you. They were willing to be frank, forthcoming, vulnerable and shed light on whatever they could. For proprietary reasons, a few asked not to be identified by name. In these cases, I use the pseudonyms "Jack" or "Jill."

A true passion project, writing this book not only helped me up my own marketing game, but allowed me to steep myself in the company of my peers and the intricacies of a career I love. I hope this book will be as enjoyable and informative for senior marketers to read as it was for me to write.

So, let's get started.

What makes the best marketing leaders tick? What qualities and practices get them excellent results and help them shine? What can we take from them to enhance our understanding of marketing and our careers? Whose model can we adapt to help us work more efficiently and effectively and serve our clients better? In short, how can we get some of that elusive and supremely potent "secret sauce"? It's a bit of a tired phrase, I know. But if you want some, read on.

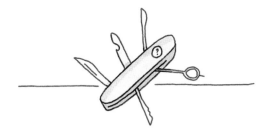

CHAPTER TWO

The Accidental Generalists

You don't know jack about Jill or Jack

I want you to meet some friends of mine: let's call them Jack and Jill. Jack and Jill are composites of the 50-plus top marketers I interviewed for this book. Jill and Jack are what successful senior marketers look like (in my mind, Jack also looks a lot like Channing Tatum, but that's just for my own entertainment).

Maybe we think we already know what "successful senior marketer" means. Maybe we think we already *are* them and that they are just like, well, *us*. As we work alongside them and observe their careers from the outside, we see professional lives that are not only flourishing but fulfilling. But what if we don't really know jack about Jack or Jill?

The Jills and Jacks interviewed for this book hail from widely varied backgrounds, pursued unique educational tracks and seemingly random career choices and were raised in different kinds of families, cultures and neighborhoods. These dynamic men and women possess certain key qualities they leverage to great advantage. The first of these you need to know about is that they are Jacks- and Jills-of-all-trades, which to the uninformed can look a little like a drawback. To the contrary, I came to learn that this trait is among their greatest strengths. They also have that very in-the-moment thing we call grit: they are resilient, meaning they risk failure and keep going. Their third key quality is that they have and share, their passion. In this chapter, we will discuss each of these attributes in depth, hear from the Jills and Jacks themselves and reflect on how we can adopt their strategies.

The first trait of a marketing superstar I want to draw your attention to is, in my opinion, woefully misunderstood in the business world. You may have heard that Jacks- and Jills-of-all-trades are generalists.

Salute the general

I remember a boss describing me as a generalist and at the time, I did not like it. I wanted to be a specialist— but now I think it is really important to BE a generalist. You do need specialists, but people who are nimble are the ones who are more inclined to grow.

Meg Goldthwaite, Chief Marketing Officer, NPR

Generalists know a little about everything, but not overly much about any *one* thing. They hold various positions within their organizations that at times do not seem to make linear sense. Some Jacks and Jills climb through the ranks of a particular company in a logical fashion. Other senior marketers jump from "agency side" to "client side." Some take an entrepreneurial jaunt, while others are labeled "creative types." This can make Jills and Jacks seem flaky, or at least unpredictable. I agree, it can look that way at first blush. In fact, many of the men and women I interviewed readily admit that they didn't take a prescribed path. They didn't necessarily fantasize about being a senior marketer from the moment they crayoned their first lemonade stand signs. Quite to the contrary, they dreamed of being actors or architects or interior designers and some even pursued those careers prior to becoming marketers. They're generalists and sometimes this gets a bad rap.

In her Forbes.com article, "'Jack of All Trades' is the Worst Possible Brand," Liz Ryan, former Fortune 500 SVP of Human Resources and author, says, "When you brand yourself as a Jack-of-all-trades, your brand turns to mush. We don't believe that a person who claims to do it all is really exceptional at any of it. Worst of all, we can't tell what you want to do in your next job. Your passion for the work you choose is the strongest part of your branding!"

However, as you will read later in this chapter, passion isn't a problem for our Jacks and Jills. And taking a while to arrive at one's vocation destination isn't necessarily a negative thing. In fact, prior to working in human resources, Ryan's own bio states she was a successful opera singer! I do understand her point, however. There are careers where a laser-like focus on a finite set of skills is essential. Specialists, like championship golfers or heart surgeons come to mind. Somehow, training for the U.S. Open part-time while spending the rest of your time perfecting your karaoke rendition of "Piano Man" doesn't increase your hole-in-one odds. By the same token, you don't want a heart surgeon who dabbles. You want a medical career that ticks all the boxes and stays on the expected trajectory—a track record of successfully doing the same thing over and over and over again with consistently excellent results.

Many of us are familiar with the importance of repeated, focused practice from Malcolm Gladwell. In his excellent book, *The Tipping Point*, Gladwell posits that it takes 10,000 hours (or approximately 10 years) of practice to gain expertise in any one thing. Marketers certainly improve with practice. We are all undoubtedly better marketers than we were 10,000 hours ago and we continue to grow. But the very nature of our field requires us to be agile in not just *one* but *any number* of different ways. My discussions with senior marketers bore this out. Many of the men and women I interviewed are what I call "accidental generalists." They fell into marketing, fell in love with it—and fellow marketers should take note of their crooked paths up the hill. I certainly did.

I never thought about marketing as a career! But I fell in love with thinking about customer-driven growth and when I got to Digitas, I realized that this is what marketing really does. There is a lot to love about marketing: it's emotional, you get stuff done and it's inherently interesting. You have a cause to go after, people who are crazy and diverse and interesting. Then you marry in technology and it becomes the "paint," a tool of the trade. [Marketing] is fascinating because it enables so much and is changing so much.

Norman de Greve, Chief Marketing Officer, CVS Health

I am here entirely by accident and happenstance. Went to college on the East Coast, decided to major in geology and be a petroleum engineer. I discovered that this would require both a master's degree and a Ph.D. and I hit a wall. I went to career services in a pursuit of a job—I knew nothing about marketing and advertising. I was afraid that someone would find me out. I put my head down and started working. I have made a point to try to hire people who have backgrounds like me. We need people with broader views and who can think constructively and critically.

Marc Ducnuigeen, Chief Operating Officer, Integer

Until my junior year in college, I changed my major three or four times. I had no idea what I wanted to do, but TV stuck with me because of internships I had. At one point I made a documentary and it occurred to me that I should do more long-form content. I really just focused on the fact that writing and producing was fun and I wanted to keep doing it. Then creative directing was fun, so I became a creative director. Then I got into managing other people. It was not a conscious decision—it was a lot of little decisions along the way.

Lara Richardson, Group Executive Vice President of Marketing, Discovery & Science Channel

noetic *note*

Is there a marketing DNA? I'm not sure. I've considered this question carefully in writing this book and will revisit the notion of innate traits versus acquired ones from different angles several times during the course of it. My gut instinct is that marketing strength, like most things, is part nature, part nurture. And I would argue that the aspects we are born with can be further developed and those we are not can most often be improved.

Take my eldest daughter, Sydney, who has gravitated toward sales and business since she was a young child. No one was more competitive in her imaginative play than she and her imagination took us to specific (work)places. Whereas other kids want to play house or school, Sydney would engage us in retail games, carefully counting her pennies, inventing office scenarios in which she, as CEO, passionately directed her subordinates (including and especially me), creating and pitching winning strategies. She is now a business major and plans to go into marketing. Was it her genes, or the fact that she grew up watching her mother run a business, overhearing client calls, seeing strategy maps spread out on the kitchen table and feeling her mother's excitement when a client was truly delighted. Or was it both?

*My father, brother and many relatives were in sales and
I think that is something in your DNA. I had a fruit stand
when I was seven years old with every intent of making good
money! I did not start at a young age with marketing. I studied
communications in college and then I fell into advertising and
liked it. So, I somewhat fell into it and somewhat I always knew.*

Rebecca Chanin, Independent Marketing Consultant

*I come from a family of marketers. My dad owned an ad agency
in Chicago and I always worked there when I was young. I
loved it and thought it was fun. But I majored in journalism
and planned to go to law school. I envisioned doing high-
profile crime work, thinking I would do the cases or report on
them. Out of school, my first job was in sales and then I ended
up in a marketing job. I always loved the creative side of it.*

**Lisa Bowman, Executive Vice President & Chief
Marketing Officer, United Way World**

*Much of what has happened in my life has been accidental.
I started my business career in the mid-1980s in the steel
industry. These were hard times in steel—not an encouraging
environment. I wanted a career change and a global company
and that is how I joined Kellogg's. [In my career], two global
consumer brand companies, Kellogg's and McDonald's, were
in need of a turnaround and I had to turn them around.
This helps you learn marketing from the ground level.*

Ken G. Kabira, Managing Principal, TrueWorks

*I kind of stumbled into it, to be honest. I was a theater major
undergrad and I really liked directing things, but I knew I
wasn't going to make a living in theater. I worked at a nonprofit
for three years and was not that passionate about it. Then I
went to a company that put me in charge of advertising. I don't*

think I realized how much I loved it until I started pitching business. Going out there and solving other people's problems was how it really got me. I never had strategic training but I was a great student [of strategy] once I got into it.

**Jan Slater, Chief Marketing Officer,
College of Business at University of Illinois**

I am an aeronautical engineer and had been in the military as a helicopter pilot. I went to a hiring conference at a hotel and Leo Burnett was there. We talked about how you can use math to support decisions and analysis to set direction and strategy. The company was in the best 100 companies and they were very clear that my math background [was an asset] and asked me to help them find opportunities. I was a geek, but the creatives also loved me.

Jack Bowen, Chief Marketing Officer, Harrison College

There was a pivotal moment when I was trying to decide if I wanted to be a graphic designer. I was tinkering, trying to determine whether I should go back to design school or get my MBA. I decided that my MBA would apply to so many things; I could still do design but needed a business understanding and this would be broader and harder working. In having done that, I feel that I am able to drive business goals as well as design logos, generate names for new products and create graphics for any purpose.

Meg Goldthwaite, Chief Marketing Officer, NPR

I fell into marketing. I have a master's degree in music composition and have never taken a marketing class. I grew up in a law family and worked in a law environment all my young years. Out of graduate school, I ended up getting an entry-level marketing role at a [law] firm and I just really enjoyed it. At that time, we were glorified party planners and it has evolved so much. I was lucky I was able to climb that ladder pretty quickly. I knew law firms so well and I was also very creative.

Liz Lockett Byrne, CMO, Miles & Stockbridge

I came into marketing pretty late in the game. I was asked to take over marketing on an interim basis. I initially said no! But my boss talked me into it. I ran marketing while I interviewed people to replace myself. It gave me a different perspective. I started reading everything I could about marketing. I sought advice. Knowing the customer, trying to deeply understand them, is fascinating to me.

Marc Solomon, Chief Marketing Officer, Threat Quotient

[In college], I had an "aha" moment when I went to a session for P&G about brand management. I went in the door not knowing what I wanted to do and walked out knowing exactly what I wanted to do. I thought it was about psychology, because I like people and find them interesting. But once I understood what brand is really about—unlocking insights about people to make business growth—it felt meant for me.

Alan Gellman, Chief Marketing Officer, Credible

I never knew what I wanted to be when I grew up and I still don't. I am passionate about ideas and solving problems. I love working with smart creative people, learning new things and having an impact and marketing combines those things.

Andrew Swinand, Chief Executive Officer, Leo Burnett

The workplace isn't the only place where specialists and generalists jockey for position and dominance with their unique skillsets; it happens in nature as well. In an article comparing specialists and generalists in nature to those in the business realm, business blogger Max Olson recognizes the strength of specialists. He explains that they thrive in the right environments because, "They fulfill a niche and are very effective at competing with other organisms." However, he argues, specialists are limited. "Generalists respond much better to changes/uncertainty. These species usually survive for very long periods because they deal with unanticipated risks better."

So, in the business world as in the natural one, we need both. This explains the symbiotic relationship between Noetic and our clients. As generalists, we help them round out their skillsets where they can—and we help them where they can't!

The willingness to embrace change benefits marketers in an industry changing at warp speed. Their "All-Tradesness" positions Jacks and Jills to succeed in the very field into which they have fallen. It is the essence of why they do what they do so well. The ability to jump around from one thing to another, then, is not a symptom of flakiness. It's not a lack of steadfastness or loyalty. It's an ability to shift gears, to be flexible. A relentless drive to learn, innovate and create—perhaps from vestiges of previous career dreams—keeps them coming back for more. And their innate passion, perseverance and resilience fuel their success. So, maybe it's not an accident after all.

Grit and the marketing genius

In her excellent and definitive book, *Grit: The Power of Passion and Perseverance*, Angela Duckworth shares a story about winning the MacArthur Fellowship, or "genius grant." As a child, Duckworth's dad told her repeatedly that she was "no genius," not out of unkindness, but perhaps to encourage humility. When she received notification of the fellowship, she imagined going back in time and conversing with him about it as a little girl.

Dad, you say I'm no genius. I won't argue with that. You know plenty of people who are smarter than I am. But let me tell you something. I'm going to grow up to love my work as much as you love yours. I won't just have a job; I'll have a calling. I'll challenge myself every day. When I get knocked down, I'll get back up. I may not be the smartest person in the room, but I'll strive to be the grittiest.

"Genius is one percent inspiration and ninety-nine percent perspiration," the inventor Thomas Edison famously said.

"It's not that I'm so smart, it's just that I stay with problems longer," Albert Einstein articulated, in what suspiciously feels like a humblebrag.

Dale Carnegie also valued "grit." "Most of the important things in the world have been accomplished by people who have kept on trying when there seemed no hope at all," he said.

For my part, I wish I had a nickel for every marketing "genius"—every Jack or Jill—who told me, "I'm not the smartest person in the room...."

They may not be the smartest, but Jills and Jacks are, in fact, often the grittiest.

noetic *note*

Grit is a key attribute I look for when hiring for Noetic. I seek out team members willing to join me in the trenches, those who will work as hard and care as deeply as I do. I've been blessed to find them. Our team is enthusiastic, passionate and tough. They work hard and play hard. We have fun, but the team instinctively knows they should give and they want to give, 100% for our clients. They actually don't know *how* to give less. We don't always get it right the first time—no one does—but we never

stop trying. I am humbled to be around them. Their
energy, steadfastness and grit make me a better leader.

As I combed the transcripts of my 50-plus Jill and Jack
interviews to write this book, three distinct facets of grit repeatedly
emerged. In fact, a whopping 83% mentioned at least one of these
ingredients as crucial to their personal secret sauce: Resilience
(30%), Willingness to Risk Failure (42%) and Passion (48%). There's
a lot to learn from how each of these talented men and women
describe and relate to their grittiness.

Let's start with the idea of *resilience*. Rebecca Chanin, former
Vice President of Marketing at JK Moving Services and currently
a marketing consultant, imagined time traveling to discuss the
concept. "I would tell my younger self that *resilience* is the best
attribute she has. You can knock me down, but I get up quickly,"
she says.

Yes, Jack and Jill carry water up the proverbial hill of the
children's rhyme. What distinguishes them is that if they fall
down on the way to the top—and most of them do at one time
or another—they darn well make sure to get back up and climb
even higher. And, to paraphrase Miley Cyrus, it's "the climb" itself
that powers them. Their uphill battle fuels their achievements and
careers.

Here's how other Jacks and Jills characterize their never-say-
die attitude:

*I have persistence: a tolerance for getting beaten up, failing,
making mistakes, acknowledging and correcting and
just getting on with things. Getting right back up. I am a
glass-half-full kind of guy. I am totally optimistic. I tend to
have a smile on my face, like to have fun and be generally*

optimistic. Particularly for Brits, this is not always the case, but I believe you have to have passion for what you do!

**Steve Hardy, Chief Marketing Officer &
Vice President, PerkinElmer, Inc.**

I don't easily take no for an answer. I think a big part of my job is that if I am told no, I ask myself who I can convince to say yes or what can I do or say to change their mind. I would tell young marketers, do everything. Don't limit yourself. When you first start out, you don't know a lot—know that. Look at everything as an opportunity.

**Lara Richardson, Group Executive Vice President
of Marketing, Discovery & Science Channel**

I am not sure why, but I am a person who is so driven. I cannot sit down for more than five minutes. No matter what role I am in, I will kill myself for you as long as you appreciate it and even when you don't! I will give it my best effort for the mission and the goal. I feel a bit like a Pied Piper. I can walk into really dysfunctional situations and work together to do our best work and set the direction.

**Amy Winter, Executive Vice President
& General Manager, UP TV**

I think there is a level of resilience in marketing, whether on the agency or client side: some things work or don't work. It is not an easy industry. The pressure is particularly high today. You used to have an annual plan and a quarterly; now the scrutiny is so much tighter. You have to have the ability to bounce back. To strike out and get back up to bat again.

Barri Rafferty, Partner & President, Ketchum

noetic *note*

When I think of not taking "no" for an answer, I can't help but think of my younger daughter, Samantha. When she was little, Sam sometimes accompanied me to the grocery store, where she would relentlessly ask for items throughout the shopping trip. No matter how many times I denied her requests, she just kept asking. I'm not talking about four or five times. I am speaking of 30 or more times in a single trip!

I am not the kind of parent who gives in after a lot of harassment. In fact, among my friends, I am famously firm, shutting down repeated requests or negotiations from little debaters with "asked and answered." But the lack of precedence that I would eventually cave did not deter Sam. Once, in an attempt to head off the incessant asking, I said at the beginning of our excursion, "I will get you *one* thing today, so decide what it is." She was about six years old at the time. She thought carefully for a moment and then responded, "Okay, Mommy. I will get one thing. But after that, I am going to keep asking for more things and you can feel free to ignore me." That's some serious self-knowledge!

As she has grown older, I have come to appreciate Sam's perseverance more and more. She will construct a case for what she wants and why it is, indeed, reasonable for me to say yes. Half the time, I am so distracted by her clever argument that I almost forget that, in whatever request she is making, she is usually fleecing me for cash!

Many of those interviewed cited hard-working parents, coaches or mentors, giving credence to the idea that Jacks and Jills both inherit and learn work ethic from their environments.

(I guess Sam had to learn this quality somewhere.) The fact is that Jacks and Jills keep going where others give up. Though they may fall down on their way up the hill, they never stop climbing. They are determined and self-motivated and won't accept "no" for an answer. This persistence is an important part of their grit.

An equally crucial piece is the ability to see avenues of opportunity where others may not. Successful senior marketers not only perceive distinct opportunities, they know that seizing them puts them in the role of change-maker. Often, they do this regardless of how high the stakes may be for them personally—and in some cases, the risk makes the challenge all the more appealing.

Risking failure—even spectacular failure—is not a stop sign for a successful senior marketer. It is a green light to keep going, persevere and accomplish more. And, importantly, Jacks and Jills evangelize a go-getter philosophy within their teams.

I push myself to get outside my comfort zone. I love doing new things and I don't worry. There are a lot of people who are smarter than I and more creative. I am a good collaborator and I can work with people well to achieve goals together.

Jeanette Cutler, Senior Director, Integrated Marketing Communications, Beam Suntory

My boss once asked me what I envisioned for myself as my next move. I thought I wanted to get into some kind of line management. She was willing to let me earn it. I raised my hand, it was scary as heck, but I got it and for the most part I am really enjoying it. I think this job will be a really pivotal point in my career. It's right now!

"Jill"

I am quite often not the smartest guy in the room. What I have is, I am not afraid of much. Not afraid to lose my job, or try something new. Perhaps I am not totally fearless, but there is not a lot that scares me from a work standpoint. So, for me, making decisions that I feel are right and appropriate, I just go with them. I will jump in and do them and this has been very helpful.

Marc Lapides, Vice President of Marketing, Communications & Programming, National Restaurant Association

I was raised on a farm in rural Oklahoma and quickly realized that luck plays a role in your success, but you have to put yourself where luck can find you. It won't come knocking on your door. You have to put yourself in places [where you can] find these opportunities. The realization of this helped me take risks.

Jerry Dow, Chief Marketing & Sales Officer, Suddenlink Communications

Any success belongs to the team; any failure is mine. This allows my people to be more creative and for me to take away some of the risk. I want my people to be risk takers. I don't want them to fear being penalized.

Jolene Nelson Helm, Principal, Astrion Partners

You cannot innovate if you are afraid to take a risk. Make sure you try to think through every possible thing that could happen and plan for it, but if something does not work, learn from it—it is not a failure. This gets harder as you get senior. When you believe in something, find a way to make it happen. [At SYFY], we tried different things within our campaigns and some worked and some did not, but we learned from all of them and would adjust.

**Sara Moscowitz, Senior Vice President,
Content Marketing & Merchandising, Audible**

*I believe what you do tomorrow is more important than
what you did yesterday. In other words, I think it is okay
to make mistakes. It does not matter. Just go forward and
do something better. No one really knows the answers, so
iterate and go forward. I don't hold onto failures at all.*

Norman de Greve, Chief Marketing Officer, CVS Health

*You have to innovate and you have to fail. I was with my team
and we were talking about a failure and I paused and said,
"Let's celebrate this failure." We test things all the time and
we fail more often than we succeed and when we succeed
that becomes our new control. Then we go back to failing to
get to the next level. I think this is an awesome philosophy.*

Alan Gellman, Chief Marketing Officer, Credible

For Jills and Jacks alike, a risk-friendly approach applies even in notably difficult situations, such as job losses, setbacks, or simply times when joy on the job is harder to find. In my 25 years of marketing, I have consistently seen job-threatening pressure increase as the marketplace continues to evolve. Companies are leaner, customer expectations are higher and the pace is faster. While you might think these dynamics would make senior marketers play it safer, I have witnessed the opposite. Successful marketers understand and remember that a setback or time of struggle is not a statement on their personal capabilities. For them, these moments call for pushing harder, believing in themselves, maintaining a learning philosophy and keeping a long-game view.

One such gritty leader—I will call him "Jack"—moved from a global media company to a global telecom a few years back. Within six weeks of his arrival, the company announced a geographic move of its headquarters and Jack's new boss promptly resigned. Jack had just relocated his family for the opportunity and now found himself with a burnt-out team and yet another city to acclimate to. When we spoke around this time, I vividly remember his words: "This is far from ideal. But the reasons I took this job are still valid and I believe I can make a difference here. This company desperately needs innovation and I know how to do that. If I can't do it, it won't be because I didn't give it my all." Three years later, the group was dramatically transformed and I am happy to say that this "Jack" and his family are happily settled.

The power of passion

Angela Duckworth argues that high achievers, or, as she calls them, accomplished "paragons of perseverance," owe much of their grit to passion.

For most, there was no realistic expectation of ever catching up to their ambitions. In their own eyes, they were never good enough. They were the opposite of complacent. And yet in a very real sense, they were satisfied with being unsatisfied. Each was chasing something of unparalleled interest and importance and it was the chase as much as the capture that was gratifying. Even if some of the things they had to do were boring, or frustrating, or even painful, they wouldn't dream of giving up. Their passion was enduring.

Political and cultural commentator David Brooks agrees that passion is vital to harnessing grit. Writing for *The New York Times*, Brooks states, "I don't know about you, but I'm really bad at being self-disciplined about things I don't care about. For me and I suspect for many, hard work and resilience can only happen when there is a strong desire. Grit is thus downstream from longing. People need a powerful *why* if they are going to be able to endure any *how*."

As I contemplate these sentiments, I cannot help but think of Leo Burnett, the founder of the Leo Burnett Company, who was a copywriter by trade and a prolific writer. His many quotes—called "Leo-isms" on the inside—shaped the culture and had an enduring effect on what is now a global company. In one of his most famous Leo-isms, he talked about "the chase" as star-reaching: "When you reach for the stars, you may not quite get one, but you won't come up with a handful of mud, either." For its entire history, Leo Burnett's leaders have made it a cornerstone of their culture to hire and grow "star reachers." This passionate dynamic permeates the halls of the agency and all its work. Marketing leaders not only understand that the act of the striving is an end in itself; they revel in it. The struggle and striving *are* the passion as they pursue an endless upside of what could be.

noetic *note*

When we at Noetic become aware of a new client opportunity, we capture the potential lead and note the key challenge to be solved. From that moment, we can't help ourselves; we get excited about divining how we can help and the prospect of digging in. Of course, as in any business, some of our leads turn into actual clients and projects and some never do. When they don't, it's not for our lack of passion. We track potential clients and stay abreast of their challenges and attempts to solve them. We stay alongside them as much as we can over time, believing we can make a

difference and knowing that, if they do call upon us, we
will work passionately to help them realize their goals.

Passion can fill a boardroom. It can call in to the conference
line. It can even permeate your PowerPoint. Passion can be a
beneficent contagion and infect everything you do in a positive
way. The passion quotient of marketing leaders I interviewed
are through the roof. They are quintessential Energizer Bunnies
who never stop beating their drums for their teams, brands and
consumers.

In *The Charisma Myth: How Anyone Can Master the Art and
Science of Personal Magnetism*, Olivia Fox Cabane describes four
types of charisma: focus, visionary, kindness and authority, each
of which demonstrate passion and enable a person to communicate
it to others. Of "visionary charisma" she says, "Visionary charisma
makes others feel inspired; it makes us believe. It can be remarkably
effective."

Cabane goes on to describe what it was like to be in the room
with a presenter with legendary magnetism. "He spoke with such
conviction, such passion. He had all of our neurons screaming,
'Yes! I get it! I'm with you!'"

*There is a childlike organic enthusiasm about many things
that I am doing. It comes across the most in person. It is a trait
that a lot of people don't have. And it is not like everyone is a
"fan," but even if you don't like me, you would still recognize
how enthusiastic and passionate I am and how into what I am
doing I am. It can be infectious and, in the right environment
and managed correctly, it can make a huge difference.*

Steven Schiffman, Chief Executive Officer, Cooper Media

*People describe me as very energetic and passionate.
When I find something awesome I want to tell everyone,
so I think I just have a knack for getting people excited
for things. I also understand peoples' trigger points, their
desire, where they want to go and how to get them there. I
have a sense for what they need and how we can solve it.*

Meg Goldthwaite, Chief Marketing Officer, NPR

*I have a ton of passion and energy and I drive for results.
What are you passionate about? An industry? A topic?
Try things and don't get locked in to one area. Don't just
think about getting promotions, try different things.
Lateral moves matter—you can learn so much from these.
Don't be afraid to take risks. Try some things and have
confidence in yourself. Look for white spaces—what do
you see not happening that should be happening?*

Alan Gellman, Chief Marketing Officer, Credible

*You need to really believe in the brand, know how to champion
it, inspiring the passion in your team and your C-suite. Give
the brand much more than the logo and a tagline. It has
to be a philosophy and a vision and how you go to market
and how you do business. It has to be like a religion.*

Jacqueline Hernández, President, MtoZ Group, LLC.

*I am always conscious about bringing energy into a room.
Always about energy, oxygen, ideas—it may sometimes
be too much, but they give me credit for energy.*

David Edelman, Chief Marketing Officer, Aetna

*I always work to find the sparkly coolness of any project I am
working on. Seeing the joy and the fun of it. To a seasoned*

marker who may feel stuck, I say, "Go find the wonder!" I know a woman who ran her first marathon at 50. If you are not in love with what you are doing, go find something else. I marketed telecom for 15 years—there is wonder in everything and our job as marketers is to find it and reveal it. I am staring at the carpet and wondering about it right now! Find the wonder; go find something amazing. Life is too short.

Meg Goldthwaite, Chief Marketing Officer, NPR

CHAPTER THREE

Elements of Excellence

By now, we've gotten to know some interesting tidbits about who our Jacks and Jills are. Let's talk for a moment about who they are not. They are not complainers. They don't spend time focusing on or fretting about how it is hard to keep up. They don't grouse about the old days, when things were simpler and marketing was more straightforward. They don't overly lament privacy issues; clutter in the marketplace; or the effort it takes to learn new platforms, apps, data and programmatic elements—or they do for a minute, then they do something about it. (I'll share some of the actions they take shortly.)

They don't whine, and they don't stand still; they just keep moving forward, seeking the technology, channels and learning that will keep them in the game. It's not that Jills and Jacks don't ever fear what's new on the horizon—of course they do, they're human—but they don't let their fear stop them. They view complacency as the enemy and curiosity and learning as their best friends.

My passion and interest is solving problems, so I love the fact that marketing is evolving and changing, because it creates new information, new technologies, new problems to solve. What is media? What is content? We are in a rapid cycle of change. It's not about fear for me. I think it's all about opportunity.

Andrew Swinand, Chief Executive Officer, Leo Burnett

We were early adopters on drones. We were the first to go out and talk to companies about how in the future they could use drones for effective assessment of safety, news, etc. We looked at this new technology and tried to figure out an opportunity to implement it.

Alina Gorokhovsky, Chief Marketing Officer, Wiley Rein LLP

In the current landscape there is so much going on, it's so complicated, so rapidly changing and anything we do can be interrupted overnight, literally. So, what is exciting is how fast we are moving.

Terry Bateman, Executive Vice President, Washington Redskins

What is pushing us? Incredibly high expectations from customers. What we are seeing is that the more digital experiences become, the more customers expect the great experience they get on Amazon to be the same in other places. They want relevance, they want to know that you know them. So, this is exciting. I have to think about how to deliver on customer expectations like this. The bar is very high. I think this will be a very exciting place for marketing and it starts to make the need for data and operations excellence so important—marketing cannot do it all on its own.

"Jill"

You may wonder if all senior marketers are this forward thinking. Maybe you worry that everyone, except perhaps you and your team, is cheerfully embracing change and adapting to the new-world marketing order without a care in the world. *I assure you this is not the case.* If you, or those around you, are anxious about the marketplace and your ability (or even desire) to keep up, you're in very good company.

noetic *note*

Many of us, including my fellow Noetic consultants and our clients, feel daunted and reticent at times. Nelson Mandela said, "The brave man is not he who does not feel afraid, but he who conquers that fear." We try to embrace this concept at Noetic: to dive into uncharted waters even when they look deep or choppy. We have developed a practice of naming and then making a point to conquer, our fears. These can be big or small, work-related or not. For example, some years ago, we identified a need to dig deeper to build our digital acumen. We sought out various avenues—some of them quite experimental—to grow our skills and create new mastery. This led to new capabilities, new projects and new momentum for our clients.

In a smaller way, we recently took a company excursion to do rock climbing. Several of us are not too wild about heights. I personally thought I was okay with heights until I actually got there and started climbing. But we've learned that recognizing and conquering fear is a path to pride and empowerment. When you experience this and practice it consistently, your hesitancy is unlocked. And, on the other side, with fear faced, you feel truly empowered.

As I interviewed more and more successful senior marketers, I realized Jills and Jacks share behaviors (as well as traits) that help them push their careers into overdrive. They:

- Displace fear with learning
- Seek out and commit to creative avenues to learn
- Strengthen both art and science sides of marketing
- Surround themselves with strong teams

These four key actions, or, as I like to call them, *The Fierce Four*," are employed with regularity to help them perform at the highest level and get maximum results. In this chapter, I will share how Jacks and Jills do these things, offering tangible examples for you to emulate and incorporate into your marketing journey and the fabric of your organization.

The Fierce Four

1. Displace fear with learning

The first of *The Fierce Four* addresses how successful senior marketers set aside fear in favor of gaining knowledge. Why do any of us fear the innovative, novel and new? It seems so silly— grown-up men and women scared of a little progress. But we are frightened. Successful senior marketers feel the exact same fear as everyone else when confronted with something innovative, strange, atypical or moving too fast. Why? Because we are all hardwired to feel that way. According to the excellent book *The 15 Commitments of Conscious Leadership: A New Paradigm for Sustainable Success*, by Jim Dethmer, Diana Chapman and Kaley Klemp, this response dates back to our cavewoman and man days, when vigilance in the face of danger was necessary to survive.

Today, while Paleo diets may be fashionable and saber-toothed tigers are no longer a threat, the innate inclination toward fearing predators and seeking safety remains. In modern times, this looks like avoiding discomfort, embarrassment and humiliation. Now, seeking safety mostly means staying within a metaphorical, rather than literal, comfort zone. Especially in a work setting, we homo sapiens want to play it safe, let someone else go first, know the answer before we contribute and cover our butts if we think we'll get called out. Think of all the meetings you've attended where there is a prompt for questions. Nine times out of ten, a full minute goes by before a brave soul raises her or his hand.

According to the authors of *15 Commitments*, all of us, regardless of upbringing or educational background, tend to work "below the line," which is defined as closed, defensive and committed to being right. We feel most secure when we feel we are "correct." We want to be good A-plus students, perceived as smart, or at least not totally stupid. I will say for myself, I simply love it when someone tells me I am right. I want to ask them to say it again, a little slower, so I can bask in this below-the-line space. But while this may *feel* like it serves us well, that's an illusion. Correctness leaves no room for learning. When we are below the line, holding on to the need to be correct, we are unable to ask critical questions and learn new things, as we're too focused on getting the right answer. We are not pursuing knowledge; we are not curious; we are not asking questions; and we are not opening ourselves to possibility and learning. In short, operating below the line may be comfortable, but it is highly limiting.

What distinguishes the men and women I interviewed for this book is their willingness to go *above* the line, cultivating a stance that is open, curious and committed to learning. It's not that they lack a normal *reaction* to reaching beyond what feels secure, but that they take constructive *action* to displace hesitancy. They acknowledge the feelings of fear or doubt—and proceed regardless. They "feel the fear and do it anyway," as Susan Jeffers advocates in her book of the same name.

"The only time you will fear anything is when you say 'no' and resist the universe," says Jeffers. "You may have heard the expression 'go with the flow.' This means consciously accepting what is happening in your life." Jacks and Jills not only understand this dynamic, they embrace it in their life as well as their life's work.

You have to get over the feeling of not wanting to ask the questions. You have to be vulnerable. Not only does it help to make yourself vulnerable and own up to what you know and don't know, but it also shapes the environment you create and the team-building that goes along with that. It is a win all the way around. Of course, you can't appear inept about everything. But assuming you bring value in other ways, it is GOOD to be vulnerable in the ways you don't know...and the whole culture will be better for it.

Pat Lafferty, President, McGarryBowen U.S.

I try to be a student of the game, to challenge myself, to go outside of my comfort zone.

David A. Wright, Chief Marketing & Commercial Officer, Minor League Baseball

I simply love learning and I believe you shouldn't worry so much about what you know and don't know. If you get a job you could do in your sleep, it's probably not the right job. Push your comfort level and your boundaries of experience. Force yourself into that new environment. You should never stagnate in your career, or in life, in order to grow with the world and the consumer. If you ever get to a point where you're no longer learning, you will lose your curiosity and your motivation.

**Ken Dice, Vice President & Global
General Manager, NikeiD, Nike**

Like Ken Dice, many senior marketers consider *curiosity* a major ally in choosing learning over fear. Another Ken cuts right to the chase:

*As soon as you start to think you are the smartest
in the room, you are in trouble. Stay curious. The
higher you climb, the more of your a** will show!*

Ken G. Kabira, Managing Principal, TrueWorks

*Curiosity is my secret sauce. I just love to solve puzzles
and understand things, whether it is data or what
is going on, I love not taking things at face value
and connecting dots. My hunger for learning and
understanding cuts across everything I have done.*

**Megan Hanley, Chief Marketing Officer,
Freedom Financial Network**

*Deep curiosity means getting in over your head, but you
have to push there and let go of your fear of failure. You
have to leap to grow. For example, when I left packaged
goods to go to health care, a key reason I made this move
was because they were doing some really interesting work
on eBusiness and I was going to lead that work. I did not
know what it was yet, but I knew it was the future. I did
it because I knew I should push myself to learn it.*

Alan Gellman, Chief Marketing Officer, Credible

I think for marketers who are successful, [the key is] curiosity and passion about how to connect with people. The best marketers are focused on this. Curiosity will drive you when no one is looking, [and help you] go the extra mile on learning the best ways to do things. It is a very different way of thinking and working.

Norman de Greve, Chief Marketing Officer, CVS Health

Curiosity is a philosophy I have always had. Growing up, [I remember when] my dad was teaching me to swim in the ocean. A wave would come and I would duck under. He taught me not to do that. He said I should stay on top and try to ride it out. I look at trends this way. I look up and see the trends and try not to duck. I try to figure out what is happening and what it means. I am always trying to learn.

Jacqueline Hernández, President of MtoZ Group, LLC

I always try to be as teachable and curious as possible. I tell myself, "I may not be the expert on this now, but I will be by the time this project is over." I have yet to come up with a challenge that I have not been able to figure out, though I do have a lot of bruises and scars, so I know with this I also have to be comfortable that there will be failure. There is a saying, "If you have a knot, patience will untie it." Meaning, if I can work on something long enough, I can figure it out. I just take it one step at a time, go get the resources I need, partner really well, garner a lot of trust, make sure everyone is in it to win it.

Meg Goldthwaite, Chief Marketing Officer, NPR

I guess I have been able to remain really humble and am always willing to learn and continue to learn. I see a lot of people my age who have shut down... they just kind of stop growing. One of my goals is to never do this and to keep learning and stay childlike.

**Terry Bateman, Executive Vice President,
Washington Redskins**

noetic *note*

In many of our trainings, we share the "above the line/below the line" philosophy and ask participants to push to work above the line during our time together. We see a distinct contrast in people's openness when encouraged to embrace curiosity over fear. It is not only productive for our collaboration; we also observe that our clients feel emotionally freed to have overt permission to learn, try and experiment.

Hearing so many talented folks liken curiosity to some kind of superpower made me more curious about its nature. I wanted to go deeper. Is curiosity something successful Jacks and Jills are given at birth, something innate? Is it something we can all develop?

According to the BBC's Tom Stafford (and science), curiosity is a characteristic all human beings share. Says Stafford in his BBC. com article, "Why Are We So Curious?":

The roots of our peculiar curiosity can be linked to a trait of the human species call neoteny... It means that as a species we are more childlike than other mammals... Evolution, by making us a more juvenile species, has made us weaker than our primate cousins, but it has also given us our child's curiosity, our capacity to learn and our deep sense of attachment to each other... Our extended childhood means we can absorb so much more from our environment.

So, the next time someone accuses you of being childish, consider it a compliment!

If survival of the fittest in the marketing jungle depends on a high dose of neoteny, what can those of us who don't feel a childlike wonder and want to enhance our curiosity do to improve? Just because it's a part of our biological destiny doesn't mean we all have it in spades. On the upside, curiosity can be nurtured to grow. In a *Psychology Today* article about cultivating curiosity, Elizabeth Svoboda has some great, tangible tips:

- Reframe "boring" situations. If you've got an inquiring mind, it's possible to turn even mundane events, like waiting in line at the DMV, into something meaningful. Look for details others might miss and seek to learn more about them.
- Don't let fear stop you from trying something new (Author's note: sound familiar?). Exercising your curiosity won't wipe out doubt, but it may help you focus on the likely positive consequences of a new venture, rather than the negative ones.
- Let your true passions shine. (Author's note: there's that word again, "passion.") A key component of curiosity is what Boston College psychologist Ellen Winner calls a "rage to master." An intense focus on specific interests or goals invites the state of mental immersion called "flow."

Another key aspect here to ramp up our learning is committing to ingesting content just to learn. Sometimes, we are so focused on our jobs and "to do list" that we rarely read an article or a book just for the sake of it. I am struck time and again how often, when I take the time to read something that simply piques my curiosity or to view a TED talk or other informative video content, what I learn comes back to enhance something I am actively working on.

A diversion from concrete projects may feel meaningless or even indulgent in the moment, but if it is inherently interesting, you are learning and you are practicing above the line curiosity. You can make your time with social media more meaningful if you take the time to read articles posted by people in your feed who you believe typically offer great content.

We are extremely fortunate that so many times we have vendors who want to come and tell us about new offerings. These can lead us in new directions. You have to do your due diligence to understand what they are trying to sell, but these are opportunities to learn and they are coming to us early on.

Nick Kelly, Head of US Sports Marketing, Anheuser-Busch InBev

2. Seek out and commit to creative avenues to learn

So, our Jacks and Jills put aside fear to learn and curiosity fuels them. *But, wait,* the old commercials tell us, *there's more.* Number 2 of *The Fierce Four* is looking for and pursuing creative ways to stay in the know. This can be the trickiest part, given a senior marketer's busy schedule, the chaos of the marketplace, the super-rapid pace of information flow and the desire to not look like a senior marketer who does not have mastery. (Yes, we want to stay above the line, but we also don't want those around us to worry about our capabilities.)

Finding innovative learning opportunities must become a specific focus. The most successful develop the habit early in their careers and curate methods that work for them—methods that include mentorship, reading, networking and testing. The senior marketers I spoke to emphasized the essential nature of a mind shift: a shift from their comfort zone toward learning new things and finding comfort with what they don't know. Or, as my yoga teacher would put it, "Finding comfort in discomfort." Senior marketers also tell me this mind shift is an everyday commitment for them and sometimes a minute-by-minute commitment. They try to be keen students of their own ignorance and compensate for their knowledge gaps in smart ways. At a practical level, how do they do this?

> "A mentor is someone who allows you to
> see the hope inside yourself."
>
> *Oprah Winfrey*

Most of my Jacks and Jills spoke reverently about their mentors' roles in their learning. They cited former bosses who took them under their wings; marketing guardian angels who appeared at key moments in their careers; and role models who are ongoing influences. I was reminded of the friendship quote so often true in my own life: "Friends come into our lives for a season, a reason or a lifetime." The same seems to be valid for mentors.

Mentors… for a season

[One of my mentors] walked in my office one day and said, "What are you working on?" I gave her more details than she needed on something she probably did not even care about, but what she did was tell me that people were noticing the work I was doing. It reminded me that when you get to that level, you should wander around. It can really fire your people up. [Another mentor] and I would sit for hours talking. We would write stuff on napkins, we have always had this kind of strategic exchange.

Jack Bowen, Chief Marketing Officer, Harrison College

I have had bosses who at times have been mentors. One boss helped me understand the importance of relationships and how to build them. I was able to watch and emulate and learn a lot this way.

Barbara Goose, SVEP & Chief Marketing Officer, John Hancock

When my boss got promoted, she asked me if I would throw my hat in the ring for her role and I had not been thinking about that at all. Then she prompted me again and I really thought about it—and I got the job. Having a boss who believes in you is really motivating, because it makes you feel like you can take some risks, sink yourself into the work and not worry about the political waters. If you are performance-oriented in the first place, this can really give you a launch pad.

Amy Winter, Executive Vice President & General Manager, UP TV

I had a couple of bosses at Quaker as I rose through the ranks who were instrumental to my success. They gave advice and counsel, but most of all they believed in me. There were also consultants who helped me. It is important to get outside your environment and these [people] were valuable in helping me understand what was happening from an outside perspective... what other companies were like and what other approaches might be within marketing.

Philip Marineau, Chairman of the Board, The Public Good Projects

My previous boss was a significant mentor for me and I was at a point in my career when the company was going through a big transformation. She saw something in me and pushed me. She was so good at giving feedback. I learned the gift of feedback from her.

"Jill"

Mentors... for a reason

My best mentors have been less about helping me understand marketing or strategy or management techniques; it has really been about emotional intelligence learning. Understanding how to deal with conflict, ambiguous situations, complex organizational structures and sophisticated board discussions... how to present oneself. If you listen and you are reasonably talented, you are going to pick things up that are very important.

Steven Schiffman, Chief Executive Officer, Cooper Media

It is always critical, when you are evaluating changing a position or leaving a company, to seek out a mentor you trust, because they know who you are and they know where you fit even better than you do. You can really learn and be more objective by listening to their point of view.

Derek Koenig, Global Head of Creative Agency, Discovery Communications

My biggest mentor was a colleague who helped me know how to really deal with people diplomatically, including staff who report to you and those you need to interact with who don't report to you. Managing people is really tricky. Most people struggle with it to some degree and you don't usually get training in this. This colleague was really amazing at it and I learned by seeing and talking to her. Mostly it was through watching her. For example, when there was something that had the potential to cause disagreement, she would be extremely prepared. Many people wing it in these moments! I was inspired and able to learn how to do this myself.

Alaina Sadick Goss, Vice President of Marketing & Communications, Strathmore

A guy I worked for in one role, I had never met such a visionary before. He was always two steps ahead of everyone else. This helped me see the whole concept of looking out on the horizon to where we could be in three to five years. I owe this skill to him.

Terry Bateman, Executive Vice President, Washington Redskins

Mentors… for a lifetime

I am fortunate that I have had a lot of mentors and most of it has happened organically—many of my bosses have been great mentors. I also have been fortunate to have transparency and openness. Not feedback once per year, but a constant discussion. It has been a really important piece [of my career] and very eye opening.

Kiera Hynninen, Associate Dean for Global Marketing and Communications, Johns Hopkins Business School

Mentors are so important. Over time they can drift into becoming peers, but it still serves you well. There are probably six to ten people from different points in my life whom I readily reach out to over time to understand their opinions on things.

Gordon Montgomery, Executive Vice President, Creative Services & Global Chief Marketing Officer, Antenna International

I love how one of our Jacks even took the time to show his mentors how much they've impacted him:

At one point, I drove to Oklahoma and found the people who had a meaningful impact on my life. I met with them and made sure I said THANK YOU to them. It was not as meaningful to them, perhaps, as it was to me, but I found my old Sunday school teacher, my old basketball coach, my cousin Bruce. The point is, people often don't know the impact they are making on your life or that you see them as a mentor until you tell them. So, I encourage people to tell this back to others.

Jerry Dow, Chief Marketing & Sales Officer, Suddenlink Communications

An interesting and effective twist on mentoring mentioned by several Jills and Jacks was the concept of "reverse mentoring." Reverse mentoring involves finding a (usually) young and savvy guide to new marketing aspects and channels. These marketers work closely with their mentor weekly, monthly, or more episodically to gain knowledge and exposure to the tech-heavy areas they do not know well. Some marketers do this within their own firm—usually behind closed doors, to keep the dynamic discreet. Others pursue a reverse mentor outside the organization to bypass the fear of looking like they don't have all the answers.

These invaluable relationships offer free-flowing learning in new and emerging platforms and key dynamics. Often such an alliance offers reciprocal mentoring for the young mentor in the form of career guidance and leadership training. Both parties serve as mentor and mentee, both getting something valuable they need.

So, you don't want to ask the dumb questions. Find a mentor in a different part of the organization. If it is functional expertise [you need], a consultant or a former employee who has retired can help. You need to find a way to learn and develop ideas without being embarrassed or losing control of the situation.

Ken Dice, Vice President & Global General Manager, NikeiD, Nike

You need to work to get reverse-mentored. For example, I was in a conversation with a data supplier and he was surprised at the questions I was asking. You don't need to be super expert, but you need to be able to ask the right questions.

Alan Gellman, Chief Marketing Officer, Credible

Reverse mentorships can be a great way to get and stay abreast and having teenagers also helps! Tapping their knowledge. The ability to ideate and know what is coming next is also super important and you have to have a passion for this.

Jeanette Cutler, Senior Director, Integrated Marketing Communications, Beam Suntory

I have a reverse mentor right now who helps me learn digital. You constantly have to be willing to open yourself up to learn new things—things I saw I did not know and I needed to learn. Sometimes I have been able to do this inside my company and sometimes I have had to go outside.

People talk about the reverse mentor, but I think it is rare how many people who do it with the rigor that I do. I have a very specific end goal in mind. For example, I wanted to build my Twitter skills. I found a person who had done this and I asked her what she needed help with. I mentored her on that and she mentored me on what I needed.

Barri Rafferty, Partner & President, Ketchum

A few years back, we decided to tap the Millennials at our agency to help us learn and help them feel empowered. The way we did this was that each of us in senior leadership was assigned a digital mentor. Once a week for one hour we got together and I would gather my questions and we would meet. We bonded and the relationship grew. I became a mentor to her and it gave me a much greater comfort factor and got me educated. I still reach out to her on these things.

Marc Ducnuigeen, Chief Operating Officer, Integer

And what if you have never had a mentor? You may be surprised to learn that several of the very successful marketers I interviewed lamented not having any mentors throughout their careers. If this is your situation, I would say two things. First, it's amazing that you got this far on only your own steam—but don't go it alone, seek this kind of input. And second, it's not too late! Mentors come from all specialties and levels within organizations. All you need to do is to look up and out to see who may be able to help you and whom you may be able to help. Start by identifying a person of promise. Invite them to coffee or lunch. Tell them you admire them and ask them how *you* can help *them*. If you start there, you are likely to gain their help.

noetic *note*

As a female business owner and mother of three—
two of whom are daughters—I look for opportunities to
help young women as often as I can. From what I observe,
young women sometimes need a bit more support and
guidance—particularly in the early years, when they
are determining what they are striving for and how to go
about it.

Our summer intern, Shannon, is a perfect example
of this. Smart and ambitious, yet unsure about what she
wants to focus on in the marketing world, we spent a
great deal of time talking about the art and science of
marketing and the importance of honing her science
side, given her strong attraction to all things art. To help
her find her footing as a young, confident marketing
executive, we spent ample time discussing charisma. It
may sound like a rote exercise, but I made Shannon do
an old-fashioned book report. She read and outlined
The Charisma Myth, by Olivia Fox Cabane (which I
cited earlier in this book), to share with our entire team.
It gave Shannon a feeling of mastery to absorb and
share what she'd learned and the content was just what
she needed at that moment in her career. There are so
many amazing tips on how to feel empowered in the
workplace and within oneself in that book. It's one of my
favorites to recommend to young female marketers.

Sometimes men have more natural swagger than women.
It's important to try to build this, to strive to have this,
to shake things off. I have had to learn not to overthink,
to learn from things, to move forward. When I drain

myself is when I overthink and blame myself. So, know how to say, "I have to learn these things," and move on.

Barri Rafferty, Partner & President, Ketchum

Another interesting way to think about mentorship, especially if you feel thin in this area, is to consider who you would invite to sit on your "personal board of directors." As Carrie Kerpen explains in her book *Work it! Secrets of Success from the Boldest of Women*, mentorship alone is not nearly as powerful as conjuring a focused, 360° network of those you feel can offer best counsel across the varied aspects of your life. Kerpen refers to these individuals as finding your FAB PAB (Fabulous Personal Advisory Board).

The way to create this FAB PAB, Kerpen explains, is to think about who you go to when you have challenges and imagine they were all on a board guiding you and your life. Who would you choose to be on that board? Kerpen emphasizes that this approach is more accessible and achievable as opposed to the traditional mentor/mentee relationship, because a personal advisory board can offer advice and support in more varied ways than a single mentor can.

Once you identify the members and make the mental commitment to have them become your circle, a key way to make this reality, as I mentioned earlier, is by first asking yourself how you can help *them*. It is critical to focus on making these relationships mutually beneficial so everyone gains value. In other words, Kerpen asks, "At whose table might I have a seat; where can I make an impact?"

Joining an organization can also be a robust way to gain your PAB and find ways to give back. To be clear, just joining will not automatically provide this connection; you need to invest the time and effort. For me, the Women Presidents Organization (WPO) has been just this kind of experience—a pivotal PAB in my professional and personal life. Some years ago, when Noetic became certified as a woman-owned business, I became eligible to join a WPO group of women business owners. I have belonged to the Washington, D.C. Chapter of WPO for four years and truly do not know what I did for advice and counsel prior to having this group.

We meet once per month and engage in a facilitated, confidential discussion of our business challenges, primarily and personal challenges, when relevant. The facilitator determines the focus of the meeting with input from the group's sharing. I walk away every time with powerful new insights on my business—and often on my life overall.

Not only is this my FAB PAB; these women are my soul sisters. We have shared the full spectrum of what life and owning a business have to offer: births, deaths, marriages, divorces, child-rearing challenges, retirement aspirations, selling of businesses, starting and endings of businesses, time management issues, talent issues, financial issues and more. We proactively look for ways to support each other and are very intentional in these asks. Often times, I have thought that, until WPO gave me water, I was dehydrated in the desert and didn't know it.

Reading, Networking and Testing

Think back to your first real job. Maybe you were fresh out of undergrad or business school and ready to take on the world. I distinctly remember what it felt like for me. I used to commute to Leo Burnett on the El (the Chicago subway). Walking the three blocks from my townhouse on Damen Avenue in Wicker Park, my '90s power suit underneath my heaviest Chicago winter coat, the *Chicago Tribune, Wall Street Journal* and *New York Times* business sections under my arm and ready to read on the commute. I can still see the ink that transferred to my tastefully neutral manicure. I can still smell the oddly inspirational scent of newsprint blended with my morning coffee. Back then, I always wanted to be water-cooler ready if talk turned to an article about clients or a supervisor wanted my take on an opinion piece. Yes, I loved a pat on the head as much as the next student. Still, this habit of continually studying our field through reading has come in handy more times than I can count over the years.

I'm sure many of us had this same practice coming up. The thing is, successful senior marketers never stop. They commit to regularly take in what's new and what's next through traditional media, Twitter, LinkedIn, online journals, podcasts… the list goes on. They also make a point to tap into youth—their own children, younger people on staff, or both—to understand what is up and coming and interesting to the next generation. The myriad ways we consume media today can be overwhelming, but it means we can read to our hearts content with no newsprint on our fingers. (Although, I will risk dating myself to ask—who doesn't still love the weight of a newspaper in their hands with a morning coffee?) Reading as much as possible, with diverse viewpoints represented, keeps you in touch with your audience—especially if they are different from you, which they often are. Reading to learn more about your audience's experience can be a big boon to your work.

I read constantly. I am a huge media consumer. I have to take the whole red state/blue state thing really seriously. [At Feed for America], we are delving to better understand the red, knowing that many of us who work here are blue, while so many of our customers are red. You cannot just assume you understand [your customer].

Catherine Davis, Chief Marketing & Communications Officer, Feeding America

*I stay abreast by staying curious—I read a lot and
pay attention to what is new. I look at what my
kids are doing, how they are communicating.*

**Jerry Dow, Chief Marketing & Sales Officer,
Suddenlink Communications**

*When a new platform comes out, you have to have people
go to it, understand what it is and how it plays in the
marketplace. You have to know how to use each platform to
its ability. This is how you stay in touch with the consumer.
You have to read constantly and you have to keep young
people around you who are participating in the platforms.
Be curious enough to understand and ask if you don't.*

Mark McIntire, Chief Marketing Officer, Roker Media

*I do a lot of reading, even though it hard to fit it in. I also
find good strategic partners to work with. I use this base
to help me think about big-picture items and strategy.*

**Jan Slater, Chief Marketing Officer,
College of Business at University of Illinois**

*For me, I am an avid reader. I am also constantly out
there talking to senior marketers and leaders. I think [our
business] is about creative solutions to problems.*

Andrew Swinand, Chief Executive Officer, Leo Burnett

As Andrew states, networking is another key practice for
our Jacks and Jills. As senior marketers, we already understand
the benefits of networking—and surely it was an essential part
of what got us where we are. It's important to remember that the
need for networking doesn't diminish for Jills and Jacks as we get
older and climb the corporate hill. In fact, it is key to keeping us

from stagnating. When we meet with people inside or outside our companies, we never know where that connection may lead. Often, we gain greater knowledge into areas where we might not otherwise have insight. Often it can lead to work, to mentors (adding to your PAB), to clients and to friends.

Some senior marketers make sure to commit to key industry events, or ask their staff to attend and bring back summaries of what they've learned. Others are lucky to have the distinct advantage of vendors pitching them new technologies, platforms and programs. By taking these meetings, they remain students of the ever-changing media landscape—and you never know who will be your next teacher and play a transformational role in your work life.

I am a voracious networker and originally committed to it as a way of growing my company and our business opportunities. While I originally pursued it for business development, the more I have networked over the years, the more I not only expand my network but nurture the network I already have and the more I realize the multitude of benefits networking provides. I am enriched by the smarts, skills and experiences people in my network share. I have any number of people I can reach out to when I have a question or a desire to connect one person to another. I am able to create a fulfilling, intellectually stimulating reunion with someone in my network in almost any city I visit. This book was an amazing exercise in expanding my network while learning from some of the best marketers in the business. I passionately believe it is critical to network for the love of learning and the connections themselves, as opposed to specific preconceived notions of what you might gain personally or professionally from a given individual.

noetic *note*

Networking from a more open, almost altruistic place, is above the line thinking at its best, or what we call at Noetic one of our core values: "Help First." When I meet or connect with someone, I focus on my genuine interest in who they are, what they do and what I might learn from them. I assess who I might connect them with, or any other way I might provide value for them. Yes, of course I am thinking about Noetic and growing our business. I know full well that this fascinating person might be someone who can help me do just that. But my focus is on the learning and I have been astounded at the people I have met and the things I have learned over the years—including and perhaps most notably from the amazing marketers I met while writing this book.

For example, I worked with a smart young woman in the Washington, D.C. area who was interested in moving to Chicago, where she had grown up. Since I have a deep network in Chicago, I connected her with several contacts. One such contact offered her a job. She took the job, moved and worked with my contact for many years as she moved up through the ranks. She recently got married and gave birth to her first child and she is loving being back in her hometown. To this day, I smile every time I think about the small role I played in her life to support a positive change she sought to make.

Networking: this is never going to be about the company you work for; it is all about the personal network you build. Your reputation is yours and yours alone.

**Amy Winter, Executive Vice President
& General Manager, UP TV**

I think that CMOs are looking to talk to other CMOs—they love to talk about themselves! They love to talk about what they have done... to share, to be very open in general, in my experience. The lifespan of a CMO can be so short. I love networking for that reason, too—because it is practical.

Colin Hall, Chief Marketing Officer & SVP, Allen Edmunds

In addition to mentoring and networking, many of the marketers I interviewed for this book consider test and learn strategies a crucial way to keep their thinking caps on. Trying a new tactic, technology or message; tracking the results; and adjusting allow them to feel emotionally and practically okay with intermediary failures on the way to more on-target approaches. The investment is small, the ability to adjust is proximate and the learning is robust. In the end, there is always a net gain, which leads to the next adjustment and frontier of effort. These days, with technology what it is, it is incredibly easy and inexpensive to employ test and learn without a large investment or a big team. You can even, as a current client of ours is doing, use Facebook groups for "AB testing," gaining almost immediate feedback, or intercept on-location testing.

[When I was head of marketing] at Art Institute of Chicago, we tested with intercepts and at times with tablets and we would always learn how to do things better. For example, we used icons to represent different genres of art to show people what could be found on a particular floor. We were having trouble getting people to the third floor. We had just one icon, because that whole floor was the same kind of art, but it turned out people were not going up because they thought there was not a lot there. When we simply added more icons, we got more people to go. You can't always know how things will be interpreted. You have to listen with an ear to optimizing.

What are people telling us that we did not anticipate?

**Gordon Montgomery, Executive Vice President,
Creative Services & Global Chief Marketing
Officer, Antenna International**

*We do a lot of test and learn. Try to carefully ask what should
we pilot and why? You end up with more of a distributed
ecosystem that learning is happening and going across.*

Norman de Greve, Chief Marketing Officer, CVS Health

*In an expanding and growing environment, you are
never going to find the next best place to expand if
you are not trying new things. You have to allocate
budget to this. It may perform worse than your core
marketing budget does, but you need to do it anyway.*

**John Swigart, Co-founder & Chief
Executive Officer, Pie Insurance**

3. Strengthen both art and science sides of marketing

Aristotle said that the whole is greater than the sum of its parts. Such is the case with our team at Noetic. In my mind's eye, I sometimes see my Noetic colleagues and myself as the many-armed Hindu goddess, Durga, her various weaponry like the many tools we bring to bear on our work. It can be exhausting trying to be everything to everyone; importantly, this should never be the goal. Within Noetic, we all have a core base of shared skills. This is important, so we can deliver with quality and consistency. Beyond that, we all have what I like to call our individual superpowers.

One teammate is amazing at design and has deep experience in video production. One was an economics major and understands market dynamics deeply and innately. Another is exceedingly resourceful and always manages to find the right content at the right time, no matter what we are trying to learn. Still another has incredible new business instincts; when we hit a bump in the road with a prospective client (who we passionately believe we can help) she instinctively knows the best approach to engage and move forward. And yet another is indefatigable in her ability to problem-solve the thorniest of operational challenges. (I could go on and on here... I love my team!) These areas of expertise in art or science are just as important as the general skills we all share.

It is not a weakness, therefore, to lead with your superpower, whether it falls on the art or science side. The men and women I interviewed are aware that being adept in art and science and strengthening their less dominant skillset, is important. And it should be comforting to note that almost no one spoke of being equally good at both. Most see themselves as stronger in one or the other.

Fascinatingly, the percentage of Jills and Jacks who saw themselves as either predominately creative or analytical was exactly the same: 38%. It is advantageous for senior marketers to make an honest assessment of their skill sets if they wish to grow. (I offer such an assessment at the end of this book). For our current purpose, let's just say #3 of *The Fierce Four* is to strive for a little bit each.

Our strength in one or the other emanates from our career beginnings and often earlier. Senior marketers who started out in agency work usually grew strong creative sides early on. Math majors who began in market research led with their analytic skills. What seems to matter now is making an effort to gain knowledge and confidence on the other side, regardless of which is naturally dominant. The marketers with whom I spoke acknowledged how very challenging and sometimes unenjoyable, that balancing act can be.

My personal story is that there was a moment in elementary school when I got a boost to my art confidence and a "ding" to my science confidence. Every year, our local grocery store in New Jersey sponsored a coloring contest prior to Easter. The coloring pages each kid did were posted on the wall behind the deli counter. Everyone colored the same scene of the Easter bunny hopping down the bunny trail. At such a young age (seven, probably), to me this seemed the equivalent of having my work displayed in a museum!

That year, as the deadline approached, I was grounded to my room for fighting with my three siblings. I was bored and thought it would be a good distraction to get my coloring piece done, but I had only a handful of markers and crayons and not in the ideal colors. Nonetheless, I completed it based on what I had on hand in my room (for example, I colored the bunny pink). I am sure you have heard the expression, "Necessity is the mother of invention." My creative expression of color, given the limited colors I had to use, won me the contest for my age group and a bucket of candy as my prize. This was huge in my world and told me I was creative at a young age. I was always writing stories and painting after that and felt like I had something to offer in the art space.

Also, in elementary school, I was a good student and worked hard. I knew I could do well if I put in the effort. In fifth grade, I was put in the most advanced math, which was actually an independent math class where the curriculum was loose—and in hindsight, as an adult, I don't think the curriculum experiment served anyone particularly well. At the time it seemed special, but when I hit sixth grade math, I struggled. I hadn't gotten some of the fundamentals that were being built upon. My teacher was very kind and had me stay after school to try to catch up, but the effect was a lack of confidence with all things numbers. This stuck with me for years and frankly, my aspiration to go to the University of Chicago for business school—the most quantitative school I knew—was in some ways an effort at redemption.

Understanding the historical underpinnings of your perceptions of your own art and science skills may help you acknowledge and address your perceived deficits. You can improve in any area you choose; it is not fixed. As we discussed in *The Fierce Four*, recognizing the fear is more than half the battle. Identifying concrete ways to address and dispel it gets you the rest of the way.

If you are more of a scientific MBA kind of marketer, you can rise up in the world of marketing to the CMO level and move outside marketing if you want. If you are more of a creative marketer, at some point you have to wrestle with the other side. As much as I pride myself on making this jump, it is hard to be as energetic about it; it requires a new context for your energy. This is the challenge in the world of marketing today: bringing together these equally powerful aspects of marketing and doing it in a way that gets to the right people to grow the business, to get the right ROIs.

**Ken Dice, Vice President & Global
General Manager, NikeiD, Nike**

You need to know and appreciate both sides. You need to be able to analyze data and patterns and understand implications. When I look at members of my team who are most successful, I think the biggest thing is the ability to take a step back and look at how a person that you are trying to reach would react to it. Being able to sit in the shoes of your target audience. Yes, in an analytical way and at the same time, with that consumer really in mind.

**Alaina Sadick Goss, Vice President of Marketing
& Communications, Strathmore**

To really succeed and elevate your career, I believe you need to be strong in both art and science. Previously, I saw people would come up in one area or the other. Now, I tend to see the digital analytics people move up in the chain. They skew toward the science side, but there is still art to their work. What is most important is that you are mindful of which you are leaning on for which decisions.

Darren Howard, Self-employed Marketing Consultant

The marketers I find to be most successful are visionary storytellers, big picture thinkers, forward thinkers. They have an eye on the consumer but are also analytical. If they only have the creative side and it is all about the splashy moment, they cannot gain traction. Being able to pivot, not holding too close to the creative, being ready to move and change. People think marketing can be very sexy, but it also can be very arduous—you have to show results. I have seen people who are "just" analytical. I think these folks tend to be very successful as long as they hire great creative agencies. They are thoughtful people making sure their investment is going far. But, they also have to make sure their teams are not just analytical. There is something in the middle; we need to be ambidextrous. We need to know when to dial up either side.

Jacqueline Hernández, President of MtoZ Group, LLC

Art and science: you have to have confidence, which needs to be based in some level of credibility. Know how to use data to test your idea before it hits the marketplace. Then, when it goes to market, if it is not successful, you still have the ability to go back and show that you did your due diligence. This is data. This is science. And, you have to be able to read the data to use judgment and make tweaks. That is the art part.

Nick Kelly, Head of US Sports Marketing, Anheuser-Busch InBev

I did well in math courses in school, but I did not necessarily like or love the numbers. When I ran our Atlanta office, I saw that the numbers really told a story: you could follow the numbers to see all kinds of things. I started to realize that embracing the data could inform a lot of things in my business decisions. Also, analytics have become so much more important and the ability to really be able to look at what is working or not working is essential. From a creativity standpoint, I have always liked that side. For me, to do just one or the other is not fulfilling.

Barri Rafferty, Partner & President, Ketchum

As a marketer yourself, you can instinctively feel which side is most comfortable for you. You may sense a subtle or profound difference. For those who lean toward artists, unlocking data or probing deeply in analysis can be challenging. Likewise, for the science-leaning among us, delivering a powerful creative idea or evaluating a design is equally daunting. Knowing there are those who are less confident on the side where we feel strong can help us feel better about our discomfort on the side where we feel less so. It's important to note that we all feel less adept on one side or the other. Imagine the excitement of unlocking the other side, even a small bit, from where you are today.

4. Surround themselves with strong teams

The first three parts of *The Fierce Four* emphasize skills that individuals can and should develop for long-term success. But our Jills and Jacks point out that they can gain immediate and long-term compensation for lack of skill on one side by building solid teams. Leaders who excel at art hire science types to round out their teams. Likewise, scientists hire creative types or add a strong agency partner to fill that role.

You've got to be comfortable recognizing your own deficiencies. I don't need another Dave Wright. I don't hire what I am and what I know. I like to build teams that can bring in other skillsets.

David A. Wright, Chief Marketing & Commercial Officer, Minor League Baseball

I believe a leader cannot be successful on his or her own. You have to work together, give credit, be surrounded by great teams with different styles. I think there is a spectrum [of art and science] and a successful team is going to have this spectrum.

Barbara Goose, SVEP & Chief Marketing Officer, John Hancock

For senior marketers you need to be a really strong leader. But just as important, you need to rely on others to bring expertise, to implement and execute with excellence. You have to know marketing well, but just as important—if not more—is finding the right people, keeping them engaged, empowering them.

Jolene Nelson Helm, Principal, Astrion Partners

At a conscious level, the thing I have learned is, every time you go up another rung, what you know and what you do is less important. It is more about your ability and willingness to surround yourself with great people and then get them to believe in a common goal and mission. My job is to be responsible for galvanizing and to bulldoze the obstacles that get in the way there.

Marc Ducnuigeen, Chief Operating Officer, Integer

I look for people who are very curious and self-aware. Understand what gaps you have in your knowledge and actively fill those gaps.

Steve Hardy, Chief Marketing Officer & Vice President, PerkinElmer, Inc.

In today's environment, it's important to collaborate with others and work in a team construct, especially if you are a marketing leader who is trying to influence other parts of marketing, so that all the different points of view can come together. The gifted marketers will surround themselves and create a team where they have people with complementary skills. If they are very analytical, they might partner with an outside agency that is extremely creative. If they are more creative, they will have strong analytics people. But a lot of times people hire far more of the same—people just like them. It is a shame when you end up with a marketing group that seems like a cult of one kind of thinking or skill.

Steven Wherenberg, Teaching Professor & Program Director, University of Minnesota

noetic *note*

As with any organizational structure, a family contains members with different skill sets. As at work, the key may be in recognizing whose skills are complementary and leveraging that for the good of the "team." Take my son Stephen, who heads off to college this year as a business major. We took the Myers-Briggs test at one point and got the complete opposite letters.

Once I saw this, it made total sense to me. He is spontaneous and outgoing, whereas I am highly planned and need time alone to refuel. He learns by doing; I learn by listening and writing out thoughts and implications. From a young age, he would disassemble an electronic device just to see what was inside and most of the time could successfully put it back together. At a practical level, having him in my household gives me a unique "home team" advantage! Not only is he a fun and wonderful son to have around, he is extremely adept at understanding how things work mechanically and fixing what is broken. I look at a glitchy TV and Wi-Fi system and know they will be in good hands with Stephen and I will be woefully understaffed in the tech department when he goes off to college this fall.

So, having complementary skills is critical to team success. It is equally important that team members share a philosophy of collective, as opposed to personal, accountability. When I first learned this concept from the business-savvy and accomplished author Patrick Lencioni, it seemed counterintuitive. Don't we want team members to feel personally accountable? As Lencioni outlines in his bestseller, *The Five Dysfunctions of a Team*, the most successful teams are focused and committed to *collective* accountability, which displaces focus on individual accomplishments.

This is a powerful governor for any team, especially teams where each individual brings his or her unique expertise. Rather than seeing oneself or another team member as the powerful one of the group with the most important skillset, each member understands and appreciates that every role enables holistic success. All succeed, or fail, together.

Lencioni shares that teams that avoid collective accountability:

- Create resentment among team members who have different standards of performance
- Encourage mediocrity
- Miss deadlines and key deliverables
- Place an undue burden on the team leader as the sole source of discipline

Teams that hold one another accountable:

- Ensure that poor performers feel pressure to improve
- Identify potential problems quickly by questioning one another's approaches without hesitation
- Establish respect among team members who are held to the same high standards
- Avoid excessive bureaucracy around performance management and corrective action

noetic *note*

At Noetic, one of our company values is, "Collaborate without egos." This was originally borne out of having a small staff and knowing that, at a practical level, each person needed to stand ready to do any task and step in at any point on any project when there was a need for an extra set of hands or a certain kind of expertise. But over the years, I have seen that the intense yet fluid collaboration we have across all clients means that every team member feels collective responsibility for the whole.

CHAPTER FOUR

Where Art Meets Science

Keep some art with the data. Don't paint by numbers.

**Steve Schiffman, a "Jack" formerly in charge
of digital for *The Washington Post***

If you've made it this far, hopefully you've learned some useful
ideas, theories and tangible actions from our Jacks and Jills. We've
talked about senior marketers from the standpoint of versatility,
or "All-Tradesness." We've looked at *The Fierce Four* actions they
take that ensure relevance. And we've begun to broach the notion
that there are art and science sides to marketing and those who can
accomplish both succeed—that in fact, a mastery of art and science
is the key force propelling senior marketers up the proverbial hill
and keeping them from coming down. In the next several chapters,
we will probe more deeply into several facets of this secret sauce
and I expect by the time we're through, you'll find yourself wanting
to sprinkle it on everything.

As we go forward, we will address what we mean when we say

"art" and "science" in this context. We will also examine how these terms relate to right- and left-brain theory and whether any of us are as one-sided as we are led to believe. We'll talk about why the current marketplace demands senior marketers who are able to shift between both, at least to some extent. We will learn how to develop each side further, playing to our strengths and compensating for our weaknesses. And, ultimately, we'll offer practical activities and tools to help you ascertain where you are in your senior marketing journey, where you can go and how to get there. But first, let's get on the same page of the sketchbook. What is art?

Art and the senior marketer

> "The artist is a receptacle for emotions that come from all
> over the place: from the sky, from the earth, from a scrap
> of paper, from a passing shape, from a spider's web."
>
> *Pablo Picasso*

We know what art is. Georgia O'Keefe painted it. Shakespeare wrote it. Alvin Ailey choreographed it. Ella Fitzgerald sang it. They were on a first-name basis with the Muse. They're artists with capital "As." When we think of imposing, hyper-successful people figures like these, art seem mysterious, cloaked in a kind of opaque elitism. What does that have to do with the rest of us? And why am I using it as a marketing term?

In its strictest definition, art is the act of creating something beautiful or meaningful. I think most of us hope there are elements of beauty and meaning in our marketing work. We may not be creating traditional masterpieces, but it's relevant. By definition, art starts with inspiration (from the Latin for "to breathe life into") and becomes any number of things. Some would argue inspiration and its transformation into something tangible, is exactly what we leverage to create behavioral change in our consumers.

Aristotle said, "The aim of art is to represent not the outward appearance of things but the inward significance." If we agree with him, art in marketing is essential. Art in marketing is less about creating something that looks or sounds good than it is about divining and projecting meaning. To do that *artfully*, we must have skills in the art realm of our field. Senior marketers who excel at art don't necessarily wield paintbrushes or even graphic design programs. They're probably not writing the pithy radio spots or sexy taglines (though some did start their careers that way). In fact, the Jacks and Jills I interviewed, even if they grew up on the art side of marketing, have risen to leadership and no longer create the creative. More often, they manage those who do.

In school, marketing artists may have gravitated toward liberal arts and studied humanities. They may have been English, history, theater, or even art majors. They often studied communications or journalism. They are people people, empathic and sensitive. They're often the natural salesmen and women among us. Frequently they come into marketing through the ad agency side of the business and some may spend their whole careers there. Many senior marketers who head down this path, though, typically get to some point where they decide they need to shift to the client side to broaden their experiences. It can be challenging for these marketers who started in art to move into science. They are aware of their need to gather skills and find thoughtful ways to do it. Jacks and Jills with an art bent have facility with the following:

- The ability to access, feel and express *emotions* effectively
- *Empathy* to read the emotions of others and the instinctive ability to effectively engage them
- An understanding and passion for *music*
- Understanding and leveraging the power of *color*
- Understanding and leveraging the power of *images*

- Understanding and leveraging the power of *words and writing*
- Perceiving and trusting one's strong intuition, *third eye, or gut instinct*
- Feeling confident in one's ability to be creative and activating *creativity* in words, images and ideas
- Confidently and prolifically *generating new ideas* and engaging with other people's ideas
- *Abstract thinking:* seeing/envisioning that which is not concrete
- *Customer-centricity:* the focus, passion and ability to deeply understand who you serve and determine how best to do so

There are so many things that you cannot get from the data. You have to witness the consumer, the questions that get asked, watching, listening, observing and balance this with the data to make sense of it all. When you are hiring someone, it is the same idea; you can see their technical skills but you also want to see their soft skills.

Lisa Bowman, Executive Vice President & Chief Marketing Officer, United Way Worldwide

No matter what, successful marketers must have an understanding of how to build great brands. The creativity that is involved in doing this can transcend platforms and distribution channels.

Amanda Cardinale, Founder & Chief Executive Officer, Workwhile

I think people need an appreciation at minimum, but ideally a strong base, of creativity. An appreciation that if it is not your forte, work with partners to leverage it. I think so much of the evolution of brands today is finding creative ways to engage and solve problems.

Andrew Swinand, Chief Executive Officer, Leo Burnett

I was interested in music and theater as a kid. I performed a lot, so that angle brought me to this industry. When I went to college, I did visual arts and thought I might want to do graphic design. I quickly realized that I wanted to not only be the person to put together the creative but to be the one to determine strategy and the concept. The more analytical side to me is also a creative outlet.

Alaina Sadick Goss, Vice President of Marketing & Communications, Strathmore

The scientific method

> "Success is a science; if you have the conditions, you get the result."
>
> *Oscar Wilde*

I am an engineer and a mathematician. [I love solving] the problem of how we find consumers and engage them that at the same time minimizes risk and gets efficiency. Most marketers are not good at math and it is really a disadvantage. If you are not good at analytics and treatment differentiation, you are just throwing darts. You have to know if what you are doing now is better than what you were doing before.

Jack Bowen, Chief Marketing Officer, Harrison College

If there is anything the internet has done, it is analytics. I think this is the true revolution in marketing. You do not have to be a statistician, but you better be versed in how to think through data and how to interface with [it].

Ken G. Kabira, Managing Principal, TrueWorks

My advice here (as a person stronger in the science side) is to become close with a data analytics person. Work at understanding where the results are coming from. Ask good questions. Most tangibly, get a good dashboard of the key analytics that are going to drive your story. It does still come back to telling stories, because the data tells a story and it is critical that you get other people to understand it. You have to make the complicated simple.

Barbara Goose, SVEP & Chief Marketing Officer, John Hancock

American astrophysicist and author Neil de Grasse Tyson says, "The very nature of science is discoveries and the best of those discoveries are the ones you don't expect." When our Jacks and Jills talk about the power of science in marketing, they are talking about the ability to predictably plan for the unpredictable, such as a consumer's reaction. To Jack Bowen's point about "throwing darts," if the desired reaction is a bulls-eye and the creative is the dart, then the science helps position the hand that sends the dart as close as possible to dead center. Acquiring and analyzing data also allows the senior marketer to maximize their follow-through and get closer to the bulls-eye the next round; testing is an important strategy for many of the senior marketers I spoke to.

With the help of science, we get the insights we need to represent the value proposition for consumers, the "why" they must believe in, purchase, or support. Science-savvy marketers might have come up more on the client side of marketing, or even begun their careers in a technical field. If life is high school writ large and the senior marketers who excel in the art of marketing are the drama club and literary magazine, then our marketing scientists are the AV club and robotics team.

Those who excel in the science side of marketing are often good at math, the sciences and finance and may have studied those subjects in school. They are more likely to have come up on the client side of marketing rather than the agency side. They need to be overt in their efforts to learn the art side. Some do this by spending time working in an agency. Others find a very strong agency partner or mentor who can help them in this area.

Straight out of my University of Chicago MBA program, I started at Leo Burnett on the Procter & Gamble account. As a fresh-faced Client Service Associate (read: lowest on the ladder), my first big assignment was to analyze Secret antiperspirant's quantitative copy-testing scores. In particular, we were having challenges with a varying "engagingness" score and the client wanted to understand why. Leveraging my science side, I dug into the copy-testing data (anyone familiar with ARS testing? If you have worked in Consumer Packaged Goods, undoubtedly you have encountered it). I looked at the numbers this way. I looked at the numbers that way. I was trying so hard to hit it out of the park on this first assignment, I memorized the numbers without even meaning to.

But, as I researched, I remembered what so many of my "quant jock" professors at University of Chicago had emphasized: ask what the data is saying. The irony of the science side of marketing is that it requires art to bring it to life. Numbers for numbers' sake will not move things forward. There must be a crafting of the story, the "so what?" to make it meaningful. (At the time, I felt it was a killer presentation, when in actual fact, it is most likely that the senior client was indulging my 25-year-old eagerness. I remember her kindness well—more than the story behind the data I created.)

Consider Amazon. Its scale and use of big data is mind-blowing—but the data itself is exhibited in such a customer-centric, story-driven manner that we feel understood, never lost in the numbers. "Deals recommended for you," "New for you," "Inspired by your wish list," and "Others who bought this also considered" help us navigate options and feel that it is about our choices, tailored for us. This is science at its best.

Jacks and Jills who are strong in the science of marketing are good at:

- Using facts and data to determine *logical* outcomes
- Using facts and data to create, prove or disprove hypotheses with *critical thinking*
- Taking comfort and mastery in numbers, formulas, data for calculation and problem solving; knowing *math*
- Demonstrating mastery in *data* identification and collection, particularly large masses of data (big data) across multiple factors
- Demonstrating mastery in *data analysis*, particularly employing large masses of data (big data) used in a coordinated fashion to draw linear conclusions
- *Linear thinking:* the ability to connect points of data and reasoning into a rational, strategic, cohesive whole
- *Business acumen:* the focus and ability to deeply understand key business dynamics that drive success, financially and strategically

The senior marketing Venn diagram

"Science is not formal logic—it needs the free play of the mind in as great a degree as any other creative art."

Physicist and mathematician Max Born

Remember the characters Chandler and Monica from the popular show *Friends*? He was a freewheeling, charismatic and hilarious guy in contrast to Monica, an adorably uptight, exceedingly organized control freak whose kitchen spices were alphabetized. And yet... they are one of the most beloved television couples of all time. Why? Because some of the best things in life happen at the intersection of seemingly opposite and complementary forces.

Now, let's look at an example of unlikely qualities peacefully co-existing in one person. Readers who are banjo fans (anyone?) are no doubt familiar with Allison Brown, a supremely talented musician. She writes and plays her own music and her dexterity with the instrument in different genres—bluegrass, Americana and Jazz—is notable. She also happens to be a Harvard grad with an MBA from UCLA. Before picking up a banjo and plucking out tunes, she worked in finance for Smith Barney.

The other day at yoga, I struck up a conversation with a woman on the mat next to me who had on a sweatshirt covered in paint spatters. When I asked her if she was a painter, she smiled and said "Only on the weekends. I am a neurologist at NIH during the week."

Up until now, we've been talking about art and science in separate silos in order to see which qualities, talents and proclivities comprise each. But what if there is more middle ground than we think, or that the pop-psychology community would have us believe? We use the terms *art* and *science*, but you may be reminded of other terms with similar polarity, such as right- and left-brained thinking, or creative versus logical. Perhaps you've taken an online quiz or two to confirm what you think you already know about yourself in these areas (there's one with a spinning ballerina that's entertaining). It's sometimes helpful and often fun to categorize ourselves as one thing or another—from determining what percent extrovert or introvert we are, to discerning whether we're (here comes another *Friends* reference) a "Ross" (total scientist, right?) or a "Phoebe" (classic artist).

The interesting thing about emerging research, however, is that right- and left-brain thinking is not as discreet or divided as we have been led to believe. According to cognitive neuroscientist Kara D. Federmeier, "There are certainly individual differences in hemispheric specialization across people, but they are very difficult to reliably determine... I think the similarities are actually more surprising than the differences."

Cognitive Psychologist David Pearson, in his article "Exploding the Myth of the Scientific vs. Artistic Mind" on www.theconversation.com, reminds us that while "stories of scientists engaging in art and vice versa are often presented as unusual," there is copious evidence to the contrary. Pearson reports that members of the Royal Society and National Academy of Sciences were almost twice as likely to engage in arts and crafts pursuits as the general public, while eminent Nobel laureate scientists were almost three times more likely to report such activities. "These findings clearly show that the stereotypical view that scientists and other logical thinkers are less likely to be artistic or creative fall wide of the mark," says Pearson. He goes on to note, "As Einstein himself noted: 'The greatest scientists are artists as well.'"

And we cannot forget Leonardo da Vinci, the ultimate Renaissance Man and perhaps the most indelible example we have of an artistic scientist—or scientific artist.

Perhaps there is no greater alchemy of art and science together than the marketing brief. Called by various names, "the brief" is a staple of the business that is at one and the same time definitive and illusive. Definitive because it is the key mechanism used to literally get everyone on the same page before a project commences, yet illusive because a tight brief is difficult to write. The adage, "If I had more time, this would be shorter," is never more true than in the brief-writing process. The best briefs, though, are the perfect melding of art and science, as they communicate the necessary data in an artful way, telling a compelling, clear story that helps everyone working from the brief not only know what is needed but feeling inspired to accomplish it.

noetic *note*

At Noetic, when we conduct training on effective brief writing, we provide a visual "brief house" that captures the core components that must hang together to tell a cohesive, inspiring story. The components themselves are equal weight art and science, as they pull from business dynamics and data, yet require a deep, empathic understanding of the customer and how we will develop communications to inspire him or her to take action that will move the business financials forward.

So, whether we're talking about brain hemispheres or spheres of greater marketing acumen, there's ample evidence that the best marketing artists and scientists can and do use both. If you look around, you will see lots of folks in daily life with unexpected and surprising talents: the hard-boiled accountant who whips up gourmet meals. The poet who kills at Sudoku puzzles. The dentist who is secretly a community theater star.

This dynamic is true for me, too. Many people know me as one who examines data, organizes things, strategizes and solves problems—typical science skills. I'm also a people person and empathetic listener who can spend hours crafting and enjoys painting (art skills). Like most people, I am not equally strong on both sides. Like our Jacks and Jills, I lean one way—in my case, toward art. In fact, when I pursued my MBA, I became a marketing and finance major. Marketing because I wanted to and finance because I felt I should (it was the University of Chicago, after all. Could I really go there and not study finance?) But knowing humans are capable of both was great news for my career and those of other senior marketers.

In his *Forbes* article, "Why Art and Science Are More Closely Related Than You Think," biology and neuroscience professor Dave Featherstone argues that not only can art and science—as well as logic and creativity—co-exist, but that they are interdependent. The success of one, he says, is essential to the success of the other:

> Scientists and artists who cannot communicate their insights are failures. It takes both skills to make a successful scientist or artist. Scientists who can communicate but have nothing new to say are frauds and hype-sters. Artists with new views of the world but who cannot communicate them effectively are crackpot fringies. Both often work hard to gain the background and skills that will help them be successful.

"Art and science are two sides of the same coin," says Jason Silva, self-described futurist, filmmaker and host of National Geographic's Brain Games.

> They ask the same questions. They look for the same answers—who are we, where did we come from, how

do things work, what does it all mean? And at times I feel like we need to let them inform one another, let the science inspire the artists and let the art tell the scientists why what they're doing matters.

You know, people only respond to what moves them and I think that's why this marriage of art and science is so crucially important, because it extends who and what we are.

Our Jills and Jacks completely agree:

To me, marketing is like a road with a fork in it: you either go toward the analytics side or the creative side. For me, I like both sides and I like the connectivity.

Lisa Bowman, Executive Vice President & Chief Marketing Officer, United Way World

I have immense respect for how difficult it is to bring together the art and science. I did not appreciate it for a long time. I believe you have to be both and you cannot do one successfully without the other. When you understand the spectrum, you are called a full stacked marketer... not everyone has appreciation of this. So, the challenge is helping organizations who think they only need one side of the equation—say the art or creative—understand that they also need science. We need to bring the context of why that matters: what it is, why it's important and how to do it.

Megan Hanley, Chief Marketing Officer, Freedom Financial Network

noetic *note*

Early on in my company, a senior marketer hired us to help clarify strategy for his marketing department. He called me in and shared his love of art—and his perceived weakness on the science side. He helped me understand that while he had a strong gut feeling of what his team needed to do to be more successful, he fully appreciated that he did not have the data to support his intuition. Together, we crafted a quantitative approach to determine his needs and priorities that led to a transformational overhaul of their internal marketing process. Once we had the data, he was delighted with the many ways it illuminated his gut instinct. He continued to appreciate his artful ability to "see it" before data had been gathered.

Around the same time, we helped another highly accomplished senior marketer launch a new go-to-market strategy that involved holding marketers more accountable for the performance and metrics of their respective businesses. When it came time to launch the process and tools, we worked closely with this leader to create and communicate compelling and inspirational brand stories. By using art (storytelling), we helped the marketing staff see the value of science (performance and metrics).

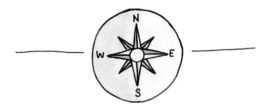

CHAPTER FIVE

The Right Method, Right Now

Driving through the landscape

As senior marketers, we talk about "the marketing landscape" a lot. Many of the Jills and Jacks I spoke with used this term. The landscape can be described as at once "crowded," "ever-changing," and "moving at the speed of light." Senior marketers hold the mythical landscape accountable for certain things that are difficult for us or others to navigate in our work. As in, "How do we serve our clients in this landscape?" Or, "How can senior marketers excel in this *landscape*?"

How do we best utilize the channels available to most meaningful and greatest impact for our customers? I'm sure I've referred to the landscape many times already in this book. We are correct to consider it. The landscape—some like to call it "marketplace"—does indeed present us with unique challenges. Let's take a minute to articulate the landscape, so we can talk about the obstacles and prospects it presents and why senior marketers use art and science to navigate both.

I find it helpful to visualize the landscape as an actual one. When I close my eyes and imagine a typical landscape, the first thing that comes to mind is a large field, maybe a pond, or some mountains in the background. I conjure the vista one sees when driving along the Pennsylvania Turnpike (though I recommend you only take this in when you are the passenger, as it is quite the winding and treacherous road with eighteen-wheelers continually speeding up to your bumper or slowing in front of you at the next incline).

I see the marketing landscape, though, more like New York City's Times Square, or the Ginza in Tokyo: exciting and fast-paced, a little overwhelming, with lots of bright, shiny things. Chaotic, colorful and crowded. Sounds and sights bombard you. Multi-media messages flash everywhere you look, competing for your attention. And a highway—the information superhighway—right down the middle, with too many on- and off-ramps going in all different directions.

Does this ring true for you?

When we talk about the landscape, we often talk about digital and technology. Many marketers I interviewed were of two minds about the state of marketing today. On the one hand, they feel novel channels and technology offer unprecedented ways to communicate with the consumer. It's a new frontier and it's invigorating. There is lot to learn and with each new platform or capability come new ways to connect meaningfully with customers. On the other hand, the Jacks and Jills take note of the sheer number of voices in the marketplace and the difficulty for their brand to be heard over the din. They also see that increasing consumer involvement in marketing means that the message is being co-created and that it can be diluted, evolved, or altogether different than the messages originally intended.

One thing is clear: the landscape poses special opportunities and challenges for our Jacks and Jills. And rising to the occasion requires a fresh approach.

Overall, it is a very exciting time. There are new things to try, to test. But it is easy to feel overwhelmed by information and technology. It is sensory overload for the marketer and a consumer. It is increasingly hard to determine what might be great versus not. It is also harder and harder to identify a point of difference as a brand; it is harder to prove. Consumers are extremely empowered and savvy. They expect high quality and value.

Rebecca Chanin, Independent Marketing Consultant

Every day you can be the first person to do X, with the channels changing all the time. At Anheuser Busch, we want to be the first brand to do anything. And you don't necessarily need a big budget to do it. We can be more creative and use nontraditional channels and still make a difference. But it is hard to know what will work, so you have to be willing to take risks with it as well, learn from what works and what doesn't.

Nick Kelly, Head of US Sports Marketing, Anheuser-Busch InBev

I think marketing had gotten a bit lost in the wilderness and I think the landscape is bringing us back to its core. I think we got lost in the t-shirts and logos and tchotchkes, the pretty things. Today, we have many more channels and routes to get to the customer. To me, this is exciting because I can make sure bets and pilot things get immediate feedback on whether they are working. In an analogue world, ten years ago, it would take me quarters and sometimes years to get to know the impact of the actions and I could not tie a particular action to a particular reaction—and now I can.

Steve Hardy, Chief Marketing Officer & Vice President, PerkinElmer, Inc.

It's both inspiring and frustrating that in today's world you are managing your brand in a different way because, truly, the public also manages your brand and they are integrated with you. Transparency is expected. Back in the day, we controlled our brands, pushed messages out and that was how we were perceived. Now you have to be part of the fabric with them and make important decisions about when you fight for yourself and when do you let your advocates do it for you. It is really exciting: where does control or influence lie? A brand is a promise still, but you're being held to even higher standards.

Kiera Hynninen, Associate Dean for Global Marketing and Communications, Johns Hopkins Business School

You look at media-consumption habits of how people process and receive information and the pace of change is overwhelming. Think about the cell phone—we check it, on average, 193 times per day. Keeping abreast and keeping ahead and understanding, but with the jet stream of data that it is being thrown off. How do you utilize it, stay ahead of it? Marketers are painfully aware of the changing consumer behavior, but if you build a "factory" then later it is obsolete, so how do you build a system that can be nimble? Do a little, learn a lot, is my philosophy. A lot of people are looking for the fully integrated system and this is a false premise. Better to try to learn and create a learning organization than try to solve it all.

Andrew Swinand, Chief Executive Officer, Leo Burnett

As much as it is important to embrace the change, marketers also warn of the tendency to be attracted to the latest "shiny object" that comes up, where they sometimes see their organizations jump before they look.

I get excited about the new shiny object, I am like a puppy that wants to see it, play with it, chew on it... I need to make sure I am evaluating it properly! Slowing down is important for me to remember. I need to stop and think. My impulsiveness can serve me well, but it can also be problematic. So, I have to be understanding of it and use it judiciously. So many shiny objects! But evaluate first.

Marc Lapides, Vice President of Marketing, Communications & Programming, National Restaurant Association

The increasingly complex marketing landscape is really fragmenting efforts. You can see it when you go to the up fronts in TV, you can see all the shiny objects, but there is no sense of what will give best result. We really need to push to know what is working the best and push for the best metrics.

Jacqueline Hernández, President of MtoZ Group, LLC

There is SO much going on in the landscape, it is so complicated, so rapidly changing and anything we are doing can be interrupted overnight, literally. What is challenging is, how do you not waste time chasing shiny objects? You have a lot of new things popping up every day; you have to wade through it to determine what will actually increase sales.

Terry Bateman, Executive Vice President, Washington Redskins

Digital marketing keeps senior marketers on their toes. McKinsey & Company talks about this continual responsiveness to the landscape as a sort of nimbleness to surviving and thriving in this time of change, when digital marketing is king. "Companies that make the deep strategic, organizational and operational shifts required to become effective digital marketers can become more agile, more productive and accelerate revenue growth," says David C. Edelman, author of the article "Four Ways to Get More Value from Digital" (on McKinsey's website) and CMO of Aetna. What do successful marketers do?

> First, they coordinate their activities to engage the consumer throughout an increasingly digital purchase journey. Second, they harness interest in their brands by syndicating content that empowers the consumer to build his or her own marketing identity and, in the process, to serve as a brand ambassador. Third, they recognize the need to think like a large-scale multimedia publisher as they manage a staggering increase in the content they create to support products, segments, channels and promotions. Finally, these marketers strategically plot how to gather and use the plethora of digital data now available.

There is no doubt that the advent and growth of digital marketing and all the channels, platforms and programs within make marketing more complex, multi-faceted and yes, more chaotic than ever before. It can be distracting for even the most seasoned marketer! And it is also important to bear in mind that digital, while a growth area, is not the only aspect of the landscape to mine. Taking the full view of our customer journey is critical to leveraging the best art and science we have to offer.

What is exciting is also concerning. There is a lot of talk of digital. To me it is the same as when e-commerce started. E-commerce was [thought of] as its own thing, when really it was just a channel. I think digital is the same way. What concerns me is the fight for people's attention. It is super hard to break through and get that moment for your brand. I think people are distracted. You have to parse it all out, figure out how to get the mind space.

Lisa Bowman, Executive Vice President & Chief Marketing Officer, United Way World

noetic *note*

At Noetic, our team often talks about how one of the greatest marketing challenges of our time in successfully managing your brand—and that the brand conversation is "always on." Consumers have the power and the access to start, end, or insert themselves into the middle of a brand conversation. Marketers who are able to run with this ever-changing dynamic are the ones who remain customer-centric and relevant. Those who do not will get left behind. Perhaps there is no better time than now to truly harness the melding of art and science to strike this balance and continue to strike it with our audiences. Staying authentic and relevant is as much about finding and leveraging the right data (science) as it is about understanding who you serve (science); what they want and need (art); and how your brand can authentically deliver this (art and science).

Another critical aspect of harnessing the power of the increasingly complex marketing landscape, but not being overtaken by it, is to leverage both art and science while being careful to lead with the customer, not with the channel.

There is a tendency of marketers to all jump on a bandwagon and go at something. For example, right now it is happening a lot with programmatic—many are investing in this and it is being described as more complicated than what it really is. I think there are a lot of eggs being put in this basket, all this investment to determine how to best serve up banner ads and online video ads. I think it is not forward-looking enough and there's probably too much focus here. I don't think it is really trying to improve the customer experience. Chatbots are in a similar place—big push by Facebook, but did not get adopted. We need to look at our business needs and figure out what is needed from there. We need to be careful to not lead with channel.

Darren Howard, Self-employed Marketing Consultant

noetic *note*

At Noetic, we often talk about "jumping to channel" as "the kangaroo effect." And while you might think kangaroos are cute, in marketing, you don't want to be one. We employ various tools with clients, such as day mapping and invoking the customer journey, to ensure that the customer's needs are at the forefront and the channels are chosen based on when, where and how we can best reach the customers. When approached this way, the ever-expanding landscape can feel less daunting, as it becomes the toolbox of tools that it really is, as opposed to an uneasy feeling that we're not trying every new platform available.

Leveraging for leadership

So, in order to build their brand and business, senior marketers must call upon all of their strengths in a crammed-full, cacophonous and sometimes confusing marketplace. We've discussed some of the ways they distinguish themselves earlier:

they have passion and grit, and rely on *The Fierce Four* key actions of successful marketers. Their ability to switch between art and science is a huge asset here—and comes in handy when our Jacks and Jills must market themselves.

Between younger marketers possessing more tech knowledge nipping at their heels and organizations wanting to do more with less, a senior marketer's desirability as a leader depends on maximizing all aspects of their skillsets. According to Inc.com, successful leaders need a mix of talents and attributes that cover quite a bit of ground.

The Inc.com article, "The Top Ten Skills Every Great Leader Needs to Succeed" cites a study by leadership experts Jack Zenger and Joseph Folkman, in which they asked more than 330,000 bosses, peers and subordinates to rank top competencies from a list of leadership skills. Interestingly, the results are a terrific mix of art and science. The list includes, but is not limited to, solving problems and analyzing issues (science); displaying technical expertise (science); and holding a strategic perspective (science)—as well as communicating powerfully (art), building relationships (art) and developing others (art).

What do Jills and Jacks say about leadership?:

Senior marketers need to be really strong leaders. You need to rely on others to bring expertise, to implement and execute with excellence. You have to know marketing well, but just as important, if not more, is finding the right people, keeping them engaged, empowering them. Know that different people are motivated differently. Yes, balance is important, but you have to have enough of the math and science part to be sure you are delivering results. You need people who are great at the art, but you cannot be a senior leader and not know your numbers, what you are delivering and how you are going to deliver. The art at a senior level is the art of persuasion and influencing. The creative art? Rarely do you need this as a senior marketer—you need this if you are a senior creative director at an agency, not a senior marketer like a CMO.

Jolene Nelson Helm, Principal, Astrion Partners

I believe you have to embrace a leadership style that is about information sharing and is open to feedback. I hate the contrived saying that you have to break down siloes, but it is so true. If you have people who are not working together, you have to force it, push them to work together. At first it is uncomfortable, especially if you come into a situation where departments are dead set against each other and you are in the middle refereeing. A lot of marketing departments are run as creative and strategy and never the two shall meet! You have to force the integration; then over time it gets easier.

Amy Winter, Executive Vice President & General Manager, UP TV

The first word I would use to describe a great leader is THOUGHTFUL. This word is not often used, as people think it means someone is soft. I don't mean that. I mean that he or she thinks things through. Really thinks through things. It is stepping back and looking at things from a holistic perspective. A lot of people think they are being evaluated on making quick decisions or tough decisions. Sure, this is a reality—at times we have to make tough decisions, but if you do them in a thoughtful way, you can look people in the eye and you can provide the rationale and thinking. People will see that you have the courage of conviction, which is very important for people to see if they are to follow you.

Rocky Romanella, Founder & Senior Partner, 3SIXTY Management Services, LLC

Daniel Goleman, in his *Harvard Business Review* article "What Makes a Leader?" heavily emphasizes the art side as being critical to a leader's success. While he notes that different situations and organizations call for different kinds of leadership,

> The most effective leaders are alike in one crucial way: they all have a high degree of what has come to be known as emotional intelligence. Without it, a person can have the best training in the world, an incisive, analytical mind and an endless supply of smart ideas, but he still won't make a great leader.

Goleman goes on to say that, for ages it has been debated whether leaders are made or born (that nature/nurture debate again). In his view, scientific inquiry offers some evidence that there is a genetic component, but that life experiences, self-awareness, maturity and the ability to learn and improve play equally critical roles. Like leadership, our abilities to grow our art and science are heavily reliant on our desire and concerted effort to do so. Take the example of emotional intelligence, a classic "art" skill. A great deal of evidence exists to show that with persistence, feedback and practice, it can be strengthened—as with any of the art and science skills. So, how can we do it?

Two of my favorite approaches on enhancing emotional intelligence in leadership are very different, but come to similar conclusions. The first is from *The 15 Commitments of Conscious Leadership: A New Paradigm for Sustainable Success*, by Jim Dethmer, Dana Chapman and Kaley Warner Klemp, to which I refer often in my work and referenced earlier regarding above the line/below the line thinking. The authors assert that when we think below the line, we are prone to participating in the Drama Triangle, in which leaders and staffs devolve into certain roles when working toward goals in a team dynamic. In the Drama

Triangle, team members become victims (who locate the cause of their experience as someone or something outside themselves); villains (who believe something is wrong and it's their job to find out who caused it); and heroes (who over-function and take more responsibility than is theirs).

One "Jack" who heads marketing at a major Midwestern hospital, warns about the danger of falling into iconic roles. "Team philosophy means getting people to work where they are best, where no one is striving to be a hero, everyone is ready to collaborate." The attraction of the Drama Triangle set-up, though and the reason it is so compelling, is that when engaged in the masquerade, those involved are fueled by adrenaline. It's oddly entertaining (as team members assume the good and bad archetypes of popular movies and books) and each actor has the benefit of feeling self-righteous—and right. Who doesn't want to feel that?

But, the authors argue, good leaders can move their teams back above the line through empathy: understanding why they and their staff are engaged in the triangle and asking themselves and others to take "radical responsibility" for their work, choices and lives—my second favorite approach. Empathy is also key to Dale Carnegie's sage advice in *How to Win Friends and Influence People*, which holds up beautifully over these many years.

Carnegie famously says that the only way under high heaven to get anyone to do anything is to make them want to. Through empathy, we are able to discern other people's wants and needs—and often what they need most is validation, to feel important. The need is almost biological. People would think it a crime to let their employees go for six days without food, Carnegie posits, but they will allow them to go six days, six weeks or even sixty years without "the hearty appreciation that they crave almost as much as they crave food."

While they look at it from different angles, each of these sources cite the importance of digging deeper within ourselves and team members. When we see behind the roles we play and access what truly makes us tick, we can perform at our best.

I am my genuine self in and outside of office. It's one of the things I take pride in and people tell me all the time—that I am the same person no matter if I am talking to the CEO or the guy who empties the waste baskets at night. I think this helps me build trust, that I am not that guy who comes out of central casting who is going to sell you some vision.

Tom Wennerberg, Executive Vice President & Marketing Director, KeyBank

Respect your people, empower your people, trust your people and always, always have their back. My approach is to create a vision and then give others the freedom to bring their own approach and style to delivering on that vision. I often talk about bringing your whole self to the role. I see my job as bringing out the best in people who work for me, not having them conform to my way of doing things.

Barri Rafferty, Partner & President, Ketchum

Liz Dolan, who is the creator and host of Satellite Sisters Podcasts and Books, leads with civility as a business philosophy:

I had someone who was an expert on civility explain to me that the three pillars of civility are: be strong, be calm, be kind. Be strong—don't let people walk all over you; be calm—don't be a yeller, no need for drama; be kind—it helps people feel better and do better. I try to move through my business life with these.

When it comes to strong leadership, the Golden Rule may be the strongest ally we have. These Jills and Jacks believe that for successful senior marketers, empathy, respect and civility must rule the day.

CHAPTER SIX

See Jack and Jill Learn

Many of us grow up believing we have certain strengths and weaknesses in the areas of art and science and I have talked a little about my own experiences in this realm. Reinforced by parents, teachers and even society's gendered ideas about who's good at what, we see ourselves as innately "not good at math" or "not creative." Sure, we all have what I would call a default strength, but to not develop the other side is a cop-out. And it's a cop-out that can cost us dearly in the actualization of our careers and lives. When marketing scientists get better at the art side, they gain skills that make them "double threats" and significantly more valuable to client teams and consumers. When the artists get comfortable with numbers and data and stop relying just on the creative to carry the day, the benefits are equally powerful. You can expand your skills for the better—but first you have to change your mind.

Integral to evolving as a marketing artist or scientist is adopting the right attitude for growth. In her illuminating book, *Mindset: The New Psychology of Success*, Carol Dweck explains how our own thoughts about our capacities can aid or inhibit our abilities to expand knowledge.

Individuals who believe their talents can be developed (through hard work, good strategies and input from others) have a growth mindset. They tend to achieve more than those with a more fixed mindset (those who believe their talents are innate gifts). This is because they worry less about looking smart and they put more energy into learning.

Dweck goes on to explain that adopting a growth mindset isn't as easy as snapping our fingers and deciding we want to learn. She argues that we all have "fixed-mindset triggers" that we must confront when we want to progress.

When we face challenges, receive criticism, or fare poorly compared with others, we can easily fall into insecurity or defensiveness, a response that inhibits growth. Our work environments, too, can be full of fixed-mindset triggers. A company that plays the talent game makes it harder for people to practice growth-mindset thinking and behavior, such as sharing information, collaborating, innovating, seeking feedback, or admitting errors.

To remain in a growth zone, we must identify and work with these triggers, says Dweck and build teams where risk-taking is encouraged. And of course, we must stay above the line in our thinking, so we can put learning before fear. Then we can begin to…

Develop art

In my discussions with our Jills and Jacks, the steps most cited to develop art in marketing are what I've nicknamed the **"Noetic 3c."**

- Staying connected with the **c**ustomer,
  or being customer-centric

- Minding your organizational **c**ulture,
  or staying culture-aware
- Nurturing an environment of exploration and
  play, which I like to call letting **c**reativity rule

I know, as many of you do, about the original 3C Model developed by Japanese organizational theorist Kenichi Ohmae. The original, important and enduring "3Cs" is an industry model that looks strategically at the factors needed for success: Company, Customers and Competitors. Only by integrating these three can a sustained competitive advantage exist. Ohmae refers to these key factors as the 3C Model, or *strategic triangle.*

Let's say the "c" of the **Noetic 3c** is perhaps a little "c" to the original big C of Ohmae's 3C Model. **Noetic 3c** can run alongside and enable you as a marketer to fully round out your art side.

It's all about the customer

Many marketers talk about customer focus. But the senior marketers I interviewed spoke more about the need for a customer-centric approach. The distinction, as spelled out in a recent article by entrepreneur and tech executive Jeremie Bacon, is that customer-focused marketing doesn't understand the value of the customer relationship *beyond a measure of revenue.* Customer-centric marketing goes further; it's about empathy—putting yourself in your customer's shoes.

There is certainly a great deal of science needed to understand and speak to your customers' needs and wants. But it is not just a "science" skill. It's not just about data. It's about comprehending where the consumer "is" and how you can meet them there. Says Bacon:

> Reaching a state of customer-centric nirvana goes
> beyond delivering what your customer wants. It requires

that you get deep into understanding their fundamental needs as part of your relationship management efforts. Organizations that are aligned around their customers seek to understand the world through their eyes.

The senior marketers I spoke with were definitively passionate on this point. Being and staying customer-centric was central for them and something they go out of their way to do. When their product was physical—brick-and-mortar-based—they extolled the virtues of walking the aisles to observe customers. When their product is virtual, or customer access was less, well, accessible, they find other creative ways of staying close to the people they serve in order to maintain and grow their empathy and customer focus over time.

In her Inc.com article, "4 Ways to Know Your Customer Better," UPS Store SVP of Marketing and Sales Michele Slykes offers these strategies for keeping the customer close:

- **Conversations.** Talk to your customers! The basic information from a survey can be helpful, but find ways to ask deeper questions. Why did they come into your store? How often do they shop for personal items? Are they finding what they are looking for? This can be a conversation in person or as a follow-up in an email or phone call. Take comfort in knowing that people like to talk about themselves—your customers will feel honored when you ask for their opinion.
- **Surveys.** Surveying customers to understand their demographic information can provide valuable insights about customer preferences. Information such as age, gender, household makeup and income can be a great place to begin. If you don't have a large budget, there are inexpensive tools available that allow you to tap into your customers.

- **Incentivize.** Sometimes people need a little push to engage. Try incentivizing customers by providing discounts or deals for their responses. A little goes a long way.
- **Branch out.** Once you know what they want, figure out the best way to give it to them. Frequently, small business owners fall into the habit of using the same marketing tools over and over because they are familiar. Or they use things they personally like. While this is understandable, it's important to meet your customer on the channel they are using.

noetic *note*

Consumer insights are a critical component of deep customer understanding and lay at the heart of any successful marketing strategy. At Noetic, when we provide training and guidance to clients on uncovering powerful insights, we emphasize that the insight represents a deeply rooted emotional want or need that you will address. Uncovering insights ensures relevance and empathy with customers.

Now let's see what our Jills and Jacks think:

For us, customers have always been the core focus. Every time we make something it is geared to this person—we call them "super-fans" and try to not just market to them but give them a full experience.

Lara Richardson, Group Executive Vice President of Marketing, Discovery & Science Channel

You have to get out of the office. Reading about a consumer is good, but you learn most when you are forced to interact. Can be ethnography, can be walking through the stores. You have to have fundamental curiosity and have to be a good conversationalist. You have to be able to chat people up and find out what they really think. And, you have to put time in. There are no short cuts.

Derek Koenig, Global Head of Creative Agency, Discovery Communications

We work to stay close to the customer and a key challenge is that when I got here they had no way to [do that]. So, I added qualitative research. I said, "Let's talk to people who are attending other cultural events." That led to a tattoo exhibit. [Discussions about] the basics of why people come and why they don't come are extremely important.

Ray DeThorne, Chief Marketing Officer, the Field Museum

I always have focus on this. Keeping frequent customer interaction, getting on the road with technicians, working a day in the store—not as an executive but as an employee—experiencing the customer and seeing the front line. At Suddenlink, I would ride with the techs on an install. Or I would sit in the call center and listen to the calls and make notes about it all.

Jerry Dow, Chief Marketing & Sales Officer, Suddenlink Communications

As an executive team we visit stores every quarter, talking to customers and employees. Also, we pull together the data we get every day with a large customer survey. We use this weekly to share customer feedback at a senior level. We take one comment every day that is reflective of what is being said, positive or negative and send it around. We also do ethnographies—these really help. Overall, it is so important to know that there is a gravitational pull on the business side and there is not this pull toward the consumer unless you are very purposeful.

Norman de Greve, Chief Marketing Officer, CVS Health

We have a big research department and we now have a lot of audience experts. Our Millennial group is Millennial and they do the research. We have a group who represent 50-plus and a group of moms who came to me and became the parenting experts. So we are trying to use research to allow people in our agency to deep dive in this vertical and not assume we know.

Barri Rafferty, Partner & President, Ketchum

All of my people have to go to the call centers, see the reps in action, how incredible they are in dealing with the questions and what the questions are. This is a big one. We also have panels where we do large-scale focus groups and pose questions and get feedback. We do also do some ethnographic work. It's very good in the way they engage people, very eye-opening and helps us unlock some different angles.

David Edelman, Chief Marketing Officer, Aetna

Often times we can get bogged down in over-analyzing stuff, so we do consumer safaris and follow consumer segments from what they do at their house to when they are out. These are self-identified avid fans or casual fans of our product, so we can understand what drives their behaviors, what the obstacles are. We also follow around competitive avid fans. We are not hitting them with a battery of questions, we are observing and it is a case-by-case. We will be a part of the group and participate with them.

Nick Kelly, Head of US Sports Marketing, Anheuser-Busch InBev

To stay really fresh and accurate of what it is like to be in [in the consumer's] shoes—I think this is a muscle you need to flex your entire life. Fortunately for me, my mom beat this into me from a very young age—"How would that make you feel?"—and got me thinking about this. Constantly thinking about the person I am channeling. It is not about changing your message—the message needs to be consistent—but being mindful of who is receiving it.

Amy Winter, Executive Vice President & General Manager, UP TV

There is a gravitational pull toward your own products. Early in my career I was involved in product marketing and you can get into navel-gazing [there]. I have long made a determined effort to put myself in the shoes of my customer and built tools and infrastructure to support this, things like customer advisory boards to get the pulse, regular qualitative and quantitative data, looking at behaviors of clients and prospects. I personally have always held myself to a high standard of spending a lot of time with sales and with customers.

Steve Hardy, Chief Marketing Officer & Vice President, PerkinElmer, Inc.

The common ground of our clients is that we go deep in the relationship to deeply understand their problems. We are constantly talking about them and their problems—both the reactive problems and proactive ones. We meet weekly and sometimes daily about problems we see in one area and how we can apply [insights] to another. We are a learning organization, because it forces us to be very connected.

Ray Steen, Chief Strategy Officer, MainSpring

noetic *note*

At Noetic, we see a gravitational pull into one's own products with every client we have ever worked with. It makes perfect sense that this would be the case. As marketers, you must be well steeped in your products or services; you live inside this environment on a daily basis. It is never going to be natural for you to be with your customers on a daily basis, unless you are physically with them. We spend a lot of time and emphasis on helping to reality-check clients on what their customers really want and need and gently remind them that these customers are not waiting for their next communication or innovation. They are going about their lives, only participating with your brands and products when it makes sense for them. Making overt efforts to be among them is the only way to stay real about customer focus and needs.

Highly cultured

Perhaps you have heard the quote often attributed to Peter Drucker, the father of modern management, "Culture eats strategy for breakfast." This is all too true and we see it happen all the time in organizations large and small. If you do not have cultural sensitivity with a deep understanding of the "currency" of the organization, you will not be successful. This is true whether you are trying to create an evolution or a revolution. People will follow if they feel you are culturally sensitive and relevant. So, in addition to keeping the customer front and center, another critical art skill is cultivating a deep understanding of your organizational culture. It's a similarly "soft" skill that requires perception and intuition, as opposed, say, logic and analysis. This is where those with a high emotional quotient, or "EQ," and the diplomats among us fare particularly well. There is much the rest of us can do to improve with a little effort.

A strong culture, in which members agree on and care intensely about organizational values, improves business performance by motivating employees and coordinating their behavior toward a vision. According to the Forbes.com article, "How Corporate Culture Can Make (Or Break) Your Organization," by Marc McClain, Founder and CEO of Sailpoint, corporate culture is becoming even more important as the modern workplace continues to evolve. "You must determine what your company's values are (or should be)," says McClain. "Then you have to use those values to evaluate each and every decision you make, including the employees you hire and the leaders you choose to represent them."

Here's what some of our culture-savvy senior marketers advise:

The right people and the right company—it starts at the top. If the values of the company and the values of your team are the same, are shared—[things] like putting new ideas on the table, being able to feel respected and valued, etc.—you will be able to be successful. If you are coming in with a different tune from what the culture sings, you will be off-key and everyone but you will see it quickly.

"Jill"

Corporate culture drives so many decisions, including the type of people who are hired. People do not realize how much culture is driving decisions that are being made. Most organizations will want to experiment with change and if it works they will want to evolve. There will be other organizations that are not looking to change and just want you to fit in. Then you have others where you have marketing neophytes who are looking for marketing leadership, but they would put you out on a limb. Then as soon as things didn't work, they might start sawing off the limb. So, you need to educate, build coalitions, understand where the real power is. You may think that you ARE the power because you come in as the senior marketer, but the real power likely lies elsewhere, with whoever is generating powerful revenue. So, you must ask where the real power lies and build bridges with them.

Steven Wherenberg, Teaching Professor & Program Director, University of Minnesota

There are big differences in the way marketing is regarded. One needs to understand what [culture] is in their organization to determine how to put things in place, based upon the philosophy. For example, in my current company, there is a lot of collaboration, so you cannot say, "This is what I want" and expect that to be successful. Just like it is in the marketplace, inside your organization you have to know what people will respond to.

Meg Goldthwaite, Chief Marketing Officer, NPR

Art Gensler is the founder of Gensler, a billion-dollar global architecture and design firm. In his book, *Art's Principles,* he writes:

Most people think that culture is what is printed in the human resources manuals that everyone must follow upon joining your firm. Culture is not about manuals. It is about setting behavior and style. Culture relates to how your team treats clients and each other. It is about how they tackle problems and create value. It concerns the presence of guiding principles that help your people do their best both at work and at home. Culture is a leadership tool. The sum total of how people apply your guiding principles and act on this mindset is your firm's culture. You will see that strong culture leads to strong performance.

One might call "behavior and style" the art of the culture. The science is what the culture produces: "strong performance."

noetic *note*

If you believe your team or department has a less-than-ideal current culture, or an undefined one, you can proactively address this challenge. Start by examining and agreeing to the values your team and department want to embody and the operating behaviors you are collectively willing to commit to and these cultural values can take root. At Noetic, we have helped many senior marketers set a new cultural course in this manner. With a growth mindset, you can spearhead this positive and powerful change. We have found it immeasurably beneficial at Noetic to deeply define our values. They guide everything we do and include:

• Dynamic positivity
• Setting the bar high
• Collaborating without egos

- Three solutions for every problem
- Curious spirit
- Help first
- Growth-minded

What values does your culture promote and practice? To get more information and insight on ours, go to: noeticconsultants.com/our-values/

Creative license

Creativity is a term often used and only vaguely understood. According to Miriam-Webster, *creativity* is the ability to make new things or think of new ideas. Creativity is very high on the senior marketers' lists of essential ingredients; for some, it's the highest.

In the world of marketing, I really believe creativity wins at the end of the day. Not necessarily "creative" but creativity overall. While there can be great data and insights and you need this, it is what I DO with it that creates marketing efforts that leave a stamp on people's minds.

Ken Dice, Vice President & Global General Manager, NikeiD, Nike

No matter what, successful marketers must have an understanding of how to build great brands. The creativity involved in doing this can transcend platforms and distribution channels. I see some people getting really savvy in certain channels, but that will only go so far.

Amanda Cardinale, Founder & Chief Executive Officer, Workwhile

I grew up with big budgets, but learning how to do something with nothing opens up the creativity. I encourage creativity—it sounds trite, but encouraging it and seeing where it will go, including small ideas that don't cost a lot but can play a role in three-dimensional impact. You have to be open and looking for these.

Gordon Montgomery, Executive Vice President, Creative Services & Global Chief Marketing Officer, Antenna International

I love the creativity and love that it looks really different every day. Because we are marketing so many different products in a given week, it is constantly changing and we have to constantly figure out how to spend our time to make the most impact.

Alaina Sadick Goss, Vice President of Marketing & Communications, Strathmore

You can think this way, too. Creative people aren't unicorns, mythical creatures touched with a gift. They're people just like you and me. Even if you have always seen yourself as a "numbers" Jill or Jack, the great news is that if you adopt the growth mindset we talked about, there are concrete things you can do to get more creative. Many of these things, by the way, are simple and *fun*.

Facing the muse-ic

A former and beloved colleague of mine, Annette Moser-Wellman, created her innovative model of creativity through a year-long study of genius. It offers insight into how creativity is inspired and can be developed. Her book, *The Five Faces of Creative Genius*, passionately extols the "democracy of creativity." Anyone, Moser-Wellman asserts, can be robustly creative if they set their focus and believe they can. She states it this way: "Most of us believe geniuses are in a league of their own. What we don't realize is that these highly creative people use skills we can all learn. People aren't geniuses; ideas are. Each of us is capable of our own breakthrough ideas."

Another way of finding the muse in our work is to find the child within. An article by Rohini Venkatraman on Inc.com, "You're 96 Percent Less Creative than You Were as a Child, Let's Reverse That," cites a NASA study that found that 98% of 1,600 four- and five-year-olds scored at "creative genius" level. Five years later, only 30% of the same group of children scored at the same level and when tested again five years later, only 12%. When the same test was administered to adults, only 2% scored at genius level. I would argue that the kindergartener is alive and well within all of us. It's time for little Jack and Jill to come out and play again—and help us raise our art sides higher.

The work of Tim Brown, CEO and president of IDEO, further supports this. In his TED talk (which has more than two million views and counting), he talks about the importance of play in creativity and how encouragement to play drops off precipitously as we leave preschool to head into higher education and later, the workplace. Brown cites the instinctive creativity of children and debunks the idea that we must leave it behind as we grow as professionals. He says:

> You can be a serious professional adult and, at times, be playful. It's not an either/or; it's an "and." You can be serious and play. So to sum it up, we need trust to play and we need trust to be creative. So, there's a connection. And there are a series of behaviors that we've learnt as kids, that turn out to be quite useful... They include exploration, which is about going for quantity; building and thinking with your hands; and role-play, where acting it out helps us both to have more empathy for the situations in which we're designing and to create services and experiences that are seamless and authentic.

Play hard to work hard

We all know what all work and no play does for Jill and Jack—so start playing more at work and see your creativity soar. Some easy strategies to try, according to Inc.com: doodling, keeping toys on your desk and taking a break to get your body moving. Moser-Wellman, in *The Five Faces of Creative Genius*, also highlights the "in-between" times in our daily lives when we are most likely to have our creative juices flowing most powerfully. This might be in the shower, before falling asleep or while in nature.

Personally, as I have come to understand and appreciate my own creativity, I have committed to focusing on these in-between times as a powerful means of thinking creatively through all sorts of business challenges toward unexpected solutions. I especially rely on daily walks with my dog as critical creative-thinking time. (As a busy business owner who needs to be efficient, this ticks so many boxes for me: exercise for me, time with my beloved dog, problem solving!)

And then there are my early mornings, when I sit with my sacred cup of coffee and no computer or handheld device yet in view. I stare into space and literally see what comes up in my mind, then capture any thoughts of consequence after the last sip is gone. This takes all of five to seven minutes and has been enormously helpful in my work as well as my personal growth. (See the Noetic Art & Science Assessment: Toolkit at the end of this book for many more concrete ideas on strengthening your creative muscles.)

noetic *note*

Recently, we conducted a qualitative study amongst individuals working in fields traditionally considered highly creative (i.e., musicians, artists, writers, film makers) to understand some of their "go to" methods of tapping their creativity. As you might imagine, they spoke eloquently of the need to overcome fear in order to create. At a practical level, the majority of these folks find that they access their most creative selves early in the day, before sleep is completely dusted off and subconscious thoughts are easier to tap. Others share that lying down at select times to either meditate or nap is the replenishment that enables them to move forward with a creative endeavor. Whatever the mode, sleep or the rested state are hyperlinked to creativity because the brain is relaxed in a different kind of way. There is tremendous scientific evidence that confirms the power of tapping into creativity through the subconscious. "Soft focus" is a key ingredient of creative output.

Develop science

Even if we were in the lowest math class in high school, senior marketers can become more adept in the science aspect of their jobs—even at a time when the technology landscape (there's that word again) is rapidly evolving. The skills on the science side of marketing—gathering data, analyzing it, approaching it from different points of view—are no less indispensable a skill to the senior marketer than being creative, culture-aware and customer-centric. Just ask our Jacks and Jills.

The main thing I have seen evolve is needing to have strong analytical chops. Not just basic math that maybe in the past you could get by with, but to be a strong marketer you have to be able to sit down with data scientists and look at models and look at customization and personalization of the customer journey. Modeling is much more important now and so you need to have rapport with data scientists. This is new versus 10 years ago.

Darren Howard, Self-employed Marketing Consultant

I talked to a guy yesterday who wants help with his analytics company—he said, "You get the data," "You get the math," "You understand how to make things efficient." This really helps me and others don't have it. At the end of the day, marketing is a hard biz and it takes a lot of rigor and analytics to market the right way and align the spending.

Jack Bowen, Chief Marketing Officer, Harrison College

More and more as marketing moves digital, we have a huge opportunity to measure our effectiveness and to make adjustments to optimize performance. [You need to] know how to take the data and insights you are getting and know what to do with them. You need modeling, data, analytics and marketing coming together in a more performance-oriented way.

"Jill"

You have to be analytical and measure. Some I think measure too much, but this is a key component. Because there is so much data and you can use it any way you choose—the key challenge is to cut through and figure out what to look at.

David Hall, Principal, the Richards Group

So, data and math are important. What do we do if we don't like numbers? What if we're more comfortable winging it, coasting along on charisma? When we get to the senior marketing level, winging no longer works. Luckily, the "**Noetic 4p**" is here to help the English majors among us up their science game.

- Hire great data **p**eople
- Commit to solid **p**reparation for you and your team

- Set thoughtful business performance measures
- Practice new skills

As with the **Noetic 3c**, it is only by happenstance that I arrived at the **Noetic 4p**, which may conjure some thought of the famous 4 Ps of Marketing. Neil Borden was the originator of the "Marketing Mix," which comprised Product, Price, Promotion and Place. These were deemed the essential ingredients to combine and capture to promote any brand. Later, another marketer coined them the Four 4 Ps, which has lasted many decades and is well known and used by marketing companies and agencies throughout the world. So once again I must specify that the "p" in **Noetic 4p** should likely be a lower-case "p," but I hope you will find them helpful.

People who need (good data) people

How do you up your game in science? Look for the smart people and have them share with you so you can learn from them. What they do, how they think—ask them all of your questions. Then you can supplement by brushing up with classes, online or offline, on data science.

Chris Schembri, Executive Director of
Marketing & Media, HCK2 Partners

It may sound obvious, but as we stated earlier in the book, building strong teams with complementary skillsets is super-important to a senior marketer's success. So, your research and data folks need to be top-notch. Crucially, they must also have enough understanding of the creative and development on the art side of marketing to facilitate cross-pollination. When building strong teams, remember to choose folks on the data side who may be math whiz kids, but also are fluent in art—people who lean toward the analytical side but can speak both languages. This combination can be hard to find. At Noetic, we often see a failure to communicate, really effectively communicate, between the analytics folks—those who have analytics in their titles—and less science-oriented marketers. Given this challenge, you, as a senior marketer, may have a unique opportunity to be the one to blend the two.

The analytics or math part has to be considered in everything that you do—it should feed a creative strategy. If you don't have that, you are missing out on a key opportunity to understand where data can send us. But don't use the data as your creative, [it should be] part of your brief, not the answer.

Marc Lapides, Vice President of Marketing, Communications & Programming, National Restaurant Association

Data is critical, you can't do almost anything without it, you better look at it hard before you make decisions. Let's say we are looking at the data to learn how to win with a preferred customer. You do a lot of analysis to then look at—who are they and where can you find them? But this does not tell you anything about what they CARE about. So, you have to push beyond the data as well, to true customer understanding.

Alan Gellman, Chief Marketing Officer, Credible

Data is a red thread that is bringing all the experiences together so that it is better for the consumer. The innovation is starting to happen a lot faster as this gets standardized, making data an ever more powerful source for consumer learning.

"Jill"

I went to a company where I was using data to build models and from here I started getting in to database marketing... and it helps you understand right person, right time, right context. Seeing the ability to connect the data-driven approach to marketing as digital was coming of age, the light bulb came on for me.

**Megan Hanley, Chief Marketing Officer,
Freedom Financial Network**

The companies that are successful today all think analytically. Inside these companies the conversation is about math. There is no precious idea, there is no, "Give us a brief and create and get feedback." It is lots of input, ideas, micro-tests, many iterations to optimize the performance and the best idea wins. It is hard to imagine that this will slow down, so if you cannot hang in this science space as a CMO today, you won't be able to 10 years from now.

**Jeff Jones, Former EVP & Chief Marketing Officer, Target;
currently President & Chief Executive Officer, H&R Block**

You have to know what you *don't* know—know where your weaknesses are and hire people who can support those areas for you. I know where my strengths and weaknesses are. I understand data and numbers; it is not my go-to, but I know it is important and put a lot of value into data-driven decisions. I have someone I can rely on to help me think through these inputs.

To put this idea to life, look at a company like Uber. Data (and stellar data people) drive every decision and every action Uber takes, from determining the supply and demand dynamically within each of its markets to helping identify which new services they will offer. Uber Pool and Uber X, as well as other services, were borne of the insights from the data.

According to Kissmetrics, Uber is storing data from every trip taken, even when the driver has no passengers. All of this data is stored and leveraged to predict supply and demand, as well as set fares. Uber looks at how transportation is handled across cities and tries to adjust for bottlenecks and other common issues. Uber also gathers data on its drivers. In addition to collecting non-identifiable information about their vehicle and location, Uber monitors their speed and acceleration and checks to see if they are working for a competing company as well (such as Lyft). As technology evolves at a way-above-the-speed-limit pace, companies must grapple with privacy issues and focus data-people power on how to protect users and themselves.

One of Uber's biggest uses of data is to inform surge pricing. This kind of dynamic pricing is similar to the pricing strategy used by hotels and airlines for weekend or holiday fares and rates, except Uber leverages predictive modeling in real-time based on traffic patterns, supply and demand. It has even been granted a patent on this type of pricing. Uber's data folks realize customers have feelings about surges. It doesn't just flippantly flick the surge switch every time it wants to make extra money. Instead, it uses data science to analyze the short- and long-term effects of surge pricing on customers. And ultimately, Uber uses an art skill—visualization—in order to make the best decisions with the information it gathers.

As with Uber and other companies we know as household names, great data people are already driving (pardon the pun) big business. In many others, data's full potential is still largely untapped. Consider, for example, CEO Randall Rothenberg's assessment of how brands are in a growth crisis, as outlined in the AdAge article, "Are You Building a 21st Century Brand?" by Steven Wolfe Pereira. Though technology has always done its part to disrupt, the brands that are harnessing data today are creating what he calls "direct" brands: brands that tap first-party data.

The traditional consumer product model is indirect. Brands rely on capital-intensive supply chains and have minimal direct interaction with customers. Here the power lies with the supply chain, retailer or whoever is able to directly aggregate and own the data. In the direct brand model, brands like Stitch Fix and Dollar Shave Club use expert data folks to create a one-on-one relationship with their customers. All the data can be captured in one place, with every transaction and interaction together. First-party data focuses wholly on the customer and their experience, with a continual loop of feedback to enable marketers to know what is on track or not. Most mind-blowing of all, while we lament about the "always on" brand conversation and how difficult it can be to "own" the brand experience, direct-party data actually enables brands to take back control of their customer relationships. This is because you are able to have a customer relationship deeper than any other brand, providing a competitive advantage to offer smarter, better and more relevant experiences.

As you might guess, these data-committed brands are deeply dedicated to performing continual A/B testing to enhance real-time discovery of how to best shape the brand and experience that customers will value highly. We all know that data and big data, are the wave of the future—and indeed, the wave is happening now. In order to leverage data best, it is important to spend time with seasoned analysts. In order to address fundamental questions about how to unlock data for the brands we are shaping, there are simply some science skills we must hire rather than develop.

Prepare, prepare, prepare

So, you hired good data folks. But what good is getting good data if you don't understand it and use it to rationalize your approach? Senior marketers who don't have a natural inclination toward numbers or data still must have the "goods" to back up their ideas, so preparation is key. And there is no greater need in the area of preparation than having a clear, well-thought-through strategy.

noetic *note*

At Noetic, we speak about strategy before execution as the preparation for the race. You have to get ready and get set before you go. In reality, many marketing folks just "go." Imagine if you did this in an actual race, without the "ready" and the "set." You might be at the track for the biggest race of your career without your shoes tied. Perhaps not facing the right way. Uncertain what distance you were running or what pace you should strive to achieve. This sounds like a very foolish way to handle a race and handling our marketing initiatives in this manner is equally foolish. Preparation means gathering the relevant data while being fully aware that you will never have perfect data. It means understanding your measurable objectives, the audience you seek to reach, how you will move them, what resources you will employ and how you will know if you have been successful.

Part of our "problem" often can be (as marketers) that we get very caught up in the tactical pieces of it. I have never cared much about what the tactics were as long as they were on strategy. I say all the time, don't get tied to the medium— worry about the message and who you serve, so you are sure to then get to the right channels. I think starting out thinking really strategically helps us rethink what we are doing.

**Jan Slater, Chief Marketing Officer,
College of Business at University of Illinois**

If you pull the strategy together properly you really cannot go wrong if you follow it or, if it does, something has changed and you have to go back and adjust for it. You have to be aware of changes—your strategy may have been right, but something changed that you have to adjust for. Getting and staying aligned keeps people aligned. It becomes like a routine purpose keeps you motivated and the distinction will have you stand out.

Jacqueline Hernández, President of MtoZ Group, LLC

My first objective and what I hold myself accountable for, is making sure there is a very insightful strategy that exists in honor of meeting whatever the marketing goals are. People use the word "strategy" so loosely. It needs to be a vision that gets pulled all the way through. It is that red thread that travels throughout (or needs to). You have a lot of tools that can allow you to measure and you need to use these strategically so you always know the big picture with the data and do not get lost in the weeds.

Jeanette Cutler, Senior Director, Integrated Marketing Communications, Beam Suntory

As Jeanette rightly states, "strategy" is bandied about often and its definition and shared understanding is murky at best. Miriam-Webster defines strategy as "a careful plan or method." While this feels accurate, it is so high-level we certainly need to drill down from the marketing perspective to get more tangible. Marketing strategy is then defined as an organization's careful plan that combines all its marketing goals into one comprehensive approach, drawing from market research data and determining the right product mix to achieve the maximum profit and sustain the business.

Michael Porter (the original *Five Forces of Marketing* creator) speaks of this murkiness and further clarifies the underpinnings of strategy in his *Harvard Business Review* article, "What is Strategy?" He writes, "The root of the problem is the failure to distinguish between operational effectiveness and strategy." Operational effectiveness is the carrying out of the method or plan, but the strategy itself must adhere to one of three commitments to deliver a cohesive marketing path:

1. Determining if you will be serving a few needs of many customers, the broad needs of few customers, or the broad needs of many customers.
2. Determining the tradeoffs you will commit to when competing: choosing what NOT to do, which is as important or more important than what you commit TO do.
3. Creating "fit" among the company's activities—aligning the activities to the strategic approach you seek to take.

As you can see, all of these require tough decisions with immense consequences, which is why data and preparation are so critical. The data and market analysis must help define this path and then help leadership and staff stick to it. Says Porter:

> Employees need guidance about how to deepen a strategic position rather than broaden or compromise it. About how to extend the company's uniqueness while strengthening the fit among its activities. This work of deciding which target group of customers and needs to serve requires discipline, the ability to set limits and forthright communication. Clearly, strategy and leadership are inextricably linked.

noetic *note*

Porter's emphasis on the importance of discipline, limit-setting and forthright communication resonate deeply with our team. Some years ago, as the leader of the company, I found myself struggling with a vision for our growth. I sought out various mentors and resources to determine how to get unstuck. I felt this was a sure case of the cobbler's kids having holes in their shoes, if a strategic marketing consultancy was unclear on its own strategy. Ultimately, via the book *Traction* and the thoughtful EOS model (and our trusted EOS advisor, Randy Taussig), we created a strategy for operational success and growth that we have committed to and honed over the years. While the initial creation of the strategy was critical and far from easy to do, just as vital is the ongoing discipline, limit-setting and commitment to communication. Or better said by the famous Peter Drucker, "Plans are only good intentions unless they immediately degenerate into hard work."

Quite often in the work we do for clients, we have these fundamental discussions because the brand or company overall is at a point of inflection. At times it is because their audience may have changed, competition may be more intense or market forces may have shifted. Sometimes, it is all of these. Higher education institutions are a keen example of this. Colleges and universities today face heavier competition as prospective students apply to more schools (and the common application making this easier). The ability to attract and retain the "right" students for the institution's goals is increasingly difficult. A critical outgrowth of this competitive heat is the need for higher education institutions to be crystal clear on their growth strategy, their audience definition and their path to achievement. Will they serve a few needs of many customers, the broad needs of few customers or the broad needs of many customers? What will they commit to do and not do? How will they align their activities to their chosen strategic path? As we have worked alongside several colleges and universities, we have plunged into existing data and sought primary data, via research, to answer these critical and fundamental questions.

Set thoughtful business performance measures

As a marketing leader, a critical part of ensuring your science is up to par is discerning and tracking the key business performance measurements that tell the story of the health of your business. Every business has the capability of distilling data to a hard-working short list of metrics that can help enlighten the recent past, diagnose the present and help set (and adjust) your course for the future.

While the specific metrics for your business heavily depend on your industry, as well as what metrics you are set up to measure and are able to access, there are best practices in this area that can help you get started or improve.

First and foremost, a critical best practice is to establish and maintain a data dashboard to measure the effectiveness across marketing activities: to track how well you and your team are meeting objectives. Importantly, the more senior you are, the more you need to have the key metrics of this dashboard align with the key metrics your peers use, so there is true alignment across disciplines to achieve company objectives.

Ideally, there will be three levels to the metrics themselves: Executive, Strategic and Tactical, according to Simon Spyer, in his article "Three Key Performance Indicators Every CEO Should

Focus On." *Executive level* is the C-Suite and CMO. Rather than the specific performance of marketing campaigns, these Key Performance Indicators (KPI) track and illuminate the commercial benefit the marketing is delivering. *Strategic level* is what the senior marketing team will want to know as topline marketing performance. This looks at things like customer behavior and high-level campaign performance. If you are on the agency side, says Spyer, this is likely what you want to focus on. And, you will want to be sure your success tracking is in sync with that of your clients. Lastly is the *tactical level*: this is handled by those delivering the specific marketing activities that you are likely overseeing. This level illuminates how specific activities are performing in market and what tactical levers may be able to be adjusted to optimize performance.

Thankfully, though the data options may seem endless and the metrics tracking will never be perfect, the core principles of business (and marketing) are very simple: sales is always a function of the number of customers you have, how often they transact with you and how much they spend on each transaction. Keeping this top of mind can help you avoid feeling overwhelmed and be used as a filter to determine the right key metrics for your level and your organization. (Look for more fodder on KPIs in our Noetic Art & Science Assessment: Toolkit.)

Practice makes (you a little bit more) perfect

The perfect PB&J has just the right ratio of peanut butter to jelly. But the right ratio depends on the person eating the sandwich. Right? (Personally, I go tend to go a bit light on the "J.") In the PB&J of your senior marketing sandwich, make sure you don't rely too much on one or the other. If you're an artful peanut butter lover, practice adding some science-boosting jelly to your senior marketing sandwich.

It can be difficult to know where and how to begin, especially when it comes to data analytics. We all know what it is conceptually, but how do we access it more tangibly and at the right level for the purposes we need? Three terrific resources that can help you get your feet wet while retaining a sense of the big picture are Google Analytics, Kissmetrics and General Assembly.

Google Analytics we have all heard of, but the Google Analytics Academy may be lesser known. It can enable you to dig in on key metrics and their meaning for your business. Kissmetrics is also well worth considering. According to HubSpot, the Kissmetrics blog can help you become well-versed in marketing analytics overall, as well as specific testing you can pursue and ways to experiment with the data you may already have. Content is posted daily so you can build your understanding of data over time in bite-sized chunks.

Lastly, you could consider e-learning courses with General Assembly. Short segments and quiz-based learning allow you to dig in on any specific question you have and go to the level of depth that suits you. General Assembly also offers live courses where you can go deep into specific science areas: big data, data science, marketing analytics and many more. Often, such course offerings may be sponsored by your company as executive learning opportunities. (For more great ways to practice good science skills, see our Noetic Art & Science Assessment: Toolkit.)

noetic *note*

When we work with clients who need to set up a dashboard, rethink their dashboard or help their teams understand how to create their own—either at a high level across initiatives or key metrics at a campaign or initiative level—we use a KPI creation tool to get to a hard-working list of metrics. Sourcing such a tool can help marketers more easily unpack not only what COULD be measured, but what SHOULD be measured to most authentically determine whether the marketing effort is meeting the business and marketing objectives. Key to this, then, is having very clear, measurable objectives. The S.M.A.R.T. approach to setting objectives is a never-fail approach to doing so, as it checks all the boxes of what a strong (SMART) objective needs to do: Be Specific, Measurable, Achievable, Results-focused and Time-bound.

Using both and knowing when to shift

Whether you lean toward peanut butter or jelly, there is tremendous value in strengthening your weaker side. In our fast-paced tech world, we will continue to need to source data while never losing sight of the art side that has and always will make marketing one of the most dynamic and innovative fields. In an industry prone to shiny objects—and as marketers likely to be dazzled by them—we need to keep one foot in the possibilities and the other firmly planted in the fundamentals of marketing that will never change. Use your head and your heart.

Another reason to strengthen your art and science is the increasing blending of the two. Take the example of two ex-agency executives who are building a tool to help companies ensure consistent branding. Companies will be able to run their assets through an automated system to ensure brand imagery follows all brand guidelines. Or consider Blaise Agüera y Arcas, principal scientist at Google, who works with deep neural networks for machine perception and distributed learning. He takes neural nets trained to recognize images and runs them in reverse to *generate* images. The results: spectacular, hallucinatory collages (and poems!) that defy categorization. Would we call it art or science? Surely, it is the complete fusion of the two.

With business moving so quickly and art and science blending, you will need to continue to hone your "All-Tradesness" to ensure a robust future. This is as much about practical skills as it is about your confidence in having them. To help with this, the assessment and toolkit that follows will enable you to determine where you fall on the spectrum of art and science and what resources, activities and tools you can source to shore up your gaps. Remember, we can develop the aspects we are born with, while those we lack can most certainly be learned. I have seen it happen in myself and others. And you will see it, too.

noetic
ART & SCIENCE
ASSESSMENT™

The best senior marketers employ a savvy combination of art and science skills. While we all come to the base camp of our careers with certain strengths, in order to scale the heights, we must assess how strong we are in each area—art or science—so we can access our superpowers and strengthen our weaknesses. There are four steps to achieving this by using our Noetic Art & Science Assessment: Toolkit.

Step 1: Take the Noetic Art & Science Assessment™, ranking yourself on each ART and SCIENCE statement from 1 to 5, where "1" means "rarely" and "5" means "always." Try to be as honest as possible, without thinking too hard about it and attempt to avoid the middle of the scale unless it is the most valid answer for you.

Step 2: Once you have answered all of the questions, add up your total ART score (maximum total points possible = 75 points) and your total SCIENCE score (maximum total points possible = 75 points). Then, subtract your total SCIENCE SCORE from your ART score to get your ART/SCIENCE BALANCE COMPOSITE SCORE.

Step 3: Once you have your number, find it within the scale descriptors to understand where you fall on the spectrum.

Step 4: Leverage the resources, activities and tools we provide to begin maximizing your art and science potential today!

ART ASSESSMENT

		1= Rarely	5= Always
1.	I believe emotions play a strong part in business and should always be considered.	1 2 3 4 5	
2.	I have a strong sense for how others are feeling, whether I am one-on-one with them or in a group.	1 2 3 4 5	
3.	I get excited when I hear other people's ideas.	1 2 3 4 5	
4.	I find that sound, rhythm, tone and other auditory cues are a powerful part of my communication and that of those around me.	1 2 3 4 5	
5.	When I want to get others excited about an idea, I like to use images to show what the end result might be. I am often most inspired when I can visualize something or am given a visual to focus on.	1 2 3 4 5	
6.	When I want to get others excited about my idea, I write about it and/or verbally explain it.	1 2 3 4 5	
7.	I believe language and wording are critical in helping convey the power of a thought or idea and I utilize this in my work.	1 2 3 4 5	
8.	I am comfortable going with my gut to make a decision.	1 2 3 4 5	
9.	I am comfortable using my imagination to see and understand possibilities.	1 2 3 4 5	
10.	I feel confident in my ability to generate new ideas on my own.	1 2 3 4 5	
11.	I feel confident in my ability to feed off the ideas of others to generate more ideas.	1 2 3 4 5	
12.	I can take seemingly disparate thoughts or ideas and link them together in unexpected ways.	1 2 3 4 5	
13.	I believe in the power of creativity and spend time cultivating it in myself and others.	1 2 3 4 5	
14.	I value the customer-centric approach and spend time strengthening it in myself and others.	1 2 3 4 5	
15.	I believe in the power and importance of storytelling and use it in my work.	1 2 3 4 5	
ADD UP YOUR TOTAL ART POINTS HERE:			

SCIENCE ASSESSMENT

	1= Rarely	5= Always

1.	I enjoy and am strong at analyzing data and drawing conclusions from it.	1 2 3 4 5
2.	I believe it is best to think a problem all the way through in a linear manner.	1 2 3 4 5
3.	I find comfort in knowing all of the facts before making a decision.	1 2 3 4 5
4.	I rely on data to determine my point of view.	1 2 3 4 5
5.	I am uncomfortable relying on gut feel when it comes to business decisions.	1 2 3 4 5
6.	I have always enjoyed math and numbers.	1 2 3 4 5
7.	I believe most problems can be solved by digging into the numbers and using logic or deductive reasoning to identify and solve for root causes.	1 2 3 4 5
8.	I am comfortable leveraging databases to analyze my business.	1 2 3 4 5
9.	I believe big data is full of opportunities and have already seen this manifest in some or most of the work I do.	1 2 3 4 5
10.	I believe numbers tell a story and it is important to uncover that story comprehensively and accurately.	1 2 3 4 5
11.	I appreciate and employ a "dashboard" of metrics to successfully diagnose and manage progress.	1 2 3 4 5
12.	I believe it is critical to define a well-crafted strategy before moving into any execution.	1 2 3 4 5
13.	I enjoy and excel at setting thoughtful strategy to drive business success.	1 2 3 4 5
14.	I am adept at understanding the big picture of the key aspects that drive business.	1 2 3 4 5
15.	I continually learn about, employ and test techniques to optimize business performance.	1 2 3 4 5
ADD UP YOUR TOTAL SCIENCE POINTS HERE:		

YOUR ART/SCIENCE BALANCE COMPOSITE:

Total ART score	+
SUBTRACT total SCIENCE score	-
YOUR ART/SCIENCE BALANCE COMPOSITE	=

SCORE ANALYSIS:

-75 to -51 = True Scientist
"Science is my jam"

You are nearly completely science-focused. You have an option here: Do you embrace your inner scientist and create a niche for yourself as a researcher, data analytics specialist or behavioral scientist? If so, double down and continue doing what you love and are most comfortable with. If, instead, you want to be more well-rounded, try some entry-level artistic things. See the Noetic Art & Science Assessment: Toolkit for resources, activities and tools you can use right away to bring ART into your life.

-50 to -26 = Leaning Toward Science
"Aspiring Einsteins"

You have strong science skills. While you may have spent some time as a creative or been creative in your youth, you may feel a bit out of touch with your art skills. Or, perhaps you question their value in our data-driven world. Honing your art skills will enable you to be the most successful marketer you can be. See the Noetic Art & Science Assessment: Toolkit for resources, activities and tools you can use right away to bring more ART into your life.

-25 to +25 = Perfectly Balanced
"My own Yin for my Yang"

Keep up the great work! To stay strong in both art and science, look for opportunities to employ both sides and shift between them, as needed. Mixing your art and science activities keeps you strong in both. See the Noetic Art & Science Assessment: Toolkit for resources, activities and tools you can use right away to help you maintain your balance.

+26 to +50 = Leaning Toward Art
"Picasso is my BAE"

You are someone who has strong art skills and feels quite comfortable in this realm. You may have grown up on the creative side, and may still reside there. You may like the idea of having more science skills, but are uncertain about how to obtain them at a practical level (and perhaps it is emotionally daunting, as well). See Noetic Art & Science Assessment: Toolkit for resources, activities and tools you can use right away to bring more SCIENCE into your life.

+51 to +75 = True Artist
"Peanut butter feels better"

You are nearly completely art-focused. You have an option here: Do you embrace your inner artist and create a niche for yourself as a designer, writer or creative? If so, double down and continue doing what you love and are most comfortable with. If, instead, you want to be more well-rounded, try some entry-level science things. See Noetic Art & Science Assessment: Toolkit for resources, activities and tools you can use right away to bring SCIENCE into your life.

How to Strengthen Art and Science Skills

The following section offer resources and activities to help strengthen your art or science skills and achieve better balance. And if you want to go deeper by learning how to use the tools I describe, Noetic Consultants can customize a training for your team's specific needs and goals.

Contact us at hello@noeticconsultants.com to learn more.

		How to Strengthen SCIENCE Skills	How to Strengthen ART Skills
		RESOURCES	
Articles/ Blogs		**Understanding KPIs** • *Marketing Profs:* "Top 5 KPIs Marketers Need" **Leveraging Marketing Data** • *Inc.:* "Overcoming CMO Challenges with Data" • *Huffington Post:* "Getting Marketing Data to Work for You" • Noetic blog post: "Research: The Foundation of a Sound Strategy" **Go-to sites for marketing data/analytics/tech inspiration** • The Moz Blog https://moz.com/blog • Neil Patel https://neilpatel.com/blog/ • Contently https://contently.com/strategist/ • Adverity https://www.adverity.com/blog • Seth Godin https://seths.blog	**Humanizing Numbers** • *Inc.:* "Connecting with Customers" **Expanding Creativity** • *Lifehack:* "Boosting Creativity" • *AdAge:* "CMOs Looking Inward for Success" **Go-to sites for creative inspiration:** • Create by Adobe https://create.adobe.com/graphic-design.html • Creative Boom https://www.creativeboom.com • Core 77 http://www.core77.com • Colossal http://www.thisiscolossal.com • My Modern Met https://mymodernmet.com • AIGA Eye on Design https://eyeondesign.aiga.org

	How to Strengthen SCIENCE Skills	How to Strengthen ART Skills
Videos	TED Talk: David McCandless, "The Beauty of Data Visualization" TED Talk: Susan Etlinger, "What Do We Do with All This Big Data" TED Talk: Kenneth Cukier, "Big Data is Better Data"	TED Talk: Elizabeth Gilbert, "Your Elusive Creative Genius" TED Talk: Drew Dudley, "Everyday Leadership" TED Talk: Tricia Wang, "The Human Insights Missing from Big Data"
Books	*The Data-Driven Marketers Strategic Playbook, Google*	*Five Faces of Creative Genius*, Annette Moser Wellman
Conferences	Most of today's conferences provide outstanding opportunities to strengthen both your art and science skills. The list below includes a host of conferences for you to consider: • AdAge Next • Adobe Summit • AMA Digital Marketing Bootcamp • AMA Marketing Week • ANA Digital and Social Media Conference • Brand Marketers Insiders Summit, MediaPost • Strategic Marketing USA, Reuters • MarketingProfs B2B Marketing Forum • Catalyst, Gartner • CSPI Connect, The Creative Problem Solving Institute • Dreamforce, SalesForce • Inbound, HubSpot • Marketing Nation Live, Marketo • SXSW	

ACTIVITIES

	How to Strengthen SCIENCE Skills	How to Strengthen ART Skills
Classes	**General Assembly, Data Analytics Courses:** Comprehensive set of data analytics courses to help you get a handle on what you should know to help you define and get the most out of your strategic marketing efforts https://generalassemb.ly/browse/data-courses-and-classes **Google Digital Garage:** Soup-to-nuts digital marketing training designed to help users harness analytics https://learndigital.withgoogle.com/digitalgarage/topic-library **HubSpot Academy:** Full suite of online training courses designed to help you leverage data, analytics and tech to drive audience engagement https://academy.hubspot.com/courses **Data-Driven Decision Making, PWC (Free via Coursera):** Online course designed to help senior marketing executives leverage the power of data to power positive outcomes http://bit.ly/JackJillDataDecisions **Positive Elearning ROL: 6 Tactics for Success** https://learning.linkedin.com/content/dam/me/learning/EMW/lil-demonstrating-positive-elearning-roi.pdf	**General Assembly, Visual Design Courses:** Comprehensive design courses from beginner through expert https://generalassemb.ly/education/visual-design **UC Davis, Content Marketing/Writing Course (via Coursera):** Powerful online course designed to help you harness creative content and content marketing tactics http://bit.ly/JackJillContentWriting **Ninja Writer's Academy:** Free timeline-driven trainings to help you master content marketing http://www.whatisaplot.com/the-ninja-writers-academy/ **Write Yourself Alive:** Creative writing intensive with a personal touch, designed to help strengthen overall writing skills while helping users overcome fear and self-doubt https://www.writeyourselfalive.org

	How to Strengthen SCIENCE Skills	How to Strengthen ART Skills
Classes (cont.)		**LinkedIn Learning's Creative Inspirations Trainings:** Ongoing documentary series offering insights from creative individuals and companies that are leaders, entrepreneurs, inventors, experts and pioneers in their fields https://www.linkedin.com/learning/search?keywords=creative%20inspirations
Actions	**Metrics:** Build a metrics dashboard that tracks the two or three main KPIs for each project you are working on. Use this at a monthly status meeting to pressure test progress. https://blog.hubspot.com/marketing/kpi-dashboard **Dashboard audit:** Do an audit of your current dashboard to pressure-test the value of what you are capturing. Challenge yourself to know how you will act on the data.	**Dive into a creative pursuit:** Take a class that uses your hands and/or body, such as cooking, painting, dancing, archery or tai chi. Let your mind wander or focus completely. Be sure to engage with the people around you as additional creative stimulus. **Hold a brainstorm:** Engage a cross-functional team in a structured brainstorm for a new project. This will help stretch your perspective of what is possible as you purposefully approach from a new direction.

	How to Strengthen SCIENCE Skills	How to Strengthen ART Skills
Actions (cont.)	**Data Analyst visits:** Seek out someone inside or outside your organization whose data skills you admire. Ask them the questions below. Do this with 2–5 different analysts to hone your own perspective and understanding. 1. What data analysis software do you find is important to be well-versed in? 2. What is your process when you start a new project? 3. What are your main focus points when designing a data-driven model to handle a business problem? 4. How do you break down time spent on analytics between data capture, reporting and analysis? 5. How do you plan to be data-driven in improving your digital marketing efforts? 6. What is your margin of error? What is an acceptable margin of error? 7. What are your favorite analytics tools and why?	**Storytelling:** Create a storytelling presentation or verbal offering based on data to tell the story of the data. **Seek the in-between space:** Commit to a specific business challenge you are having where you need fresh ideas. With that in mind, go for a walk, practice yoga, clean a closet, do yardwork or do something with your body that requires mental concentration OUTSIDE of your work problem. Allowing your body to move will give your subconscious the space it needs to mull the problem. Capture ideas as needed. **Embrace visualization:** Taking a specific example in hand, present a data analysis and findings to an individual or your team using only pictures. **Writing/Journaling:** Carve time to sit down and write the challenges you want to solve, and the ideas you have for solving them. Use words and pictures. Let your thoughts flow without judging them. Commit to doing this a few times a week without any distractions. Revisit these pages to see what you may want to act on. Keep the journal on hand so you can pick it up when an idea strikes you, and take the moment to capture it.

How to Strengthen SCIENCE Skills	TOOLS	How to Strengthen ART Skills
Business Situation to Draft Marketing Objective Tool (BSMO): Helps you sift through data to find the aspects most relevant to the business situation you are focused on, then develop potential objectives for your initiative		**Brief House:** Don't just focus on the KPIs; make sure your briefs hang together and tell an inspiring and focused story that will motivate
SMART Objective Worksheet: Provides a structure for setting well-thought-out, measurable objectives		**4 Whys:** You love finding interesting facts. Now dig under those facts to uncover unmet needs and desires of your target audience—also known as customer insights
Marketing Objective Refinement Tool: Enables you to move from a draft marketing objective to a finalized, specific, measurable objective		**Customer Insight Checklist:** Provides an objective, customer-centric view of whether you have reached a deep, meaningful insight
KPI Distillation Framework: Helps you diverge to explore possible metrics, then focus on the one to three metrics that will best track your objectives		**Messaging Matrix:** Open your mind and diverge on different messaging options that can fulfill an identified customer insight
Strategic Marketing Research Checklist: A robust checklist of the types of resources you can access to ensure you are strategically investigating your initiative		**Customer Day Mapping:** Puts you in the seat of your target audience to determine their daily activities and media habits as preparation for thoughtful channel selection that marries data with customer-centric thinking
Test & Learn Checklist: Enables you to brainstorm what you *could* test and learn for an initiative, then distill to what you *should* test and learn		**Customer Journal Tool:** Helps you identify the stage of the journey you most need to affect with a given campaign or your overall strategy; and determine the best actions and channels for this need

How to Strengthen SCIENCE Skills	How to Strengthen ART Skills
Research Plan Worksheet: Provides a framework for a research plan to ensure you gain the data and learning necessary to meet your objectives	**STRONG Creative Evaluator:** Use this set of questions to guide your thinking for nurturing strong creative
Data Curation Questionnaire: An interrogation that enables discernment between what data you have gathered and what data you still need to move forward	**Storytelling Framework:** Learn how to turn stats and facts into compelling stories
Google Search Tips & Tricks: A helpful list of ways to get the most from your Google data searches	**"Science to Art" Tool:** A diagnostic tool that helps you sift through data to determine point-of-view options and hypotheses
Marketing Brief Checklist: This hearty checklist ensures you are building the strongest brief for your marketing communications initiative	
PESTL Analysis Worksheet: Assists you to interrogate the macro trends affecting your industry and your company	
Customer Segmentation Readiness: This checklist helps you determine if you and your organization are in need of a segmentation and are ready to conduct and activate one successfully	If you want to go deeper by learning how to use the tools I describe, Noetic Consultants can customize a training for your team's specific needs and goals. Visit noeticconsultants.com for more information.
SWOT Analysis Worksheet: Helps you determine the Strengths, Weaknesses, Opportunities and Threats of a situation, as well as what implications to draw from them	

Four Years Later...

INTRO TO
New Chapters

When I wrote this book in the Before Times, one of the last sentences read: With business moving so quickly and art and science blending, you will need to continue to hone your "All-Tradesness" to ensure a robust future.

Now close to 2023, I did not know how true this would be. As we navigate a world that continues to change before our eyes, we need our All-Tradesness now more than ever. We need adaptability, a passion for learning and acceptance of fear. We need to focus on the here and now, to let go of expectations yet make plans and strategies without knowing if they have a good chance of coming to fruition. We need to hold everything loosely, yet hold it all the same.

Over the last three years we have seen, experienced and endured many things we never imagined. I continue to run my company (there were some moments in 2020 when I wondered if I still could), and I continue to see marketers scale the heights despite so many new obstacles in their paths. Given these extraordinary times, I decided to revisit the efforts of these leaders by following up with those I had spoken to before, and speaking with marketing leaders I met during the last few years who I saw surviving and thriving. I wanted to understand in their view and in their own words, what was still true, what was more true, what was newly true -- since the Before Times. I wanted to understand this from extraordinary leaders who see their life and their work as always learning, and always scaling.

For my part, I started the March 2020 shutdown helping my older children get home from their spring break trips in Mexico before the borders closed, navigating the chaos that had become my business and also navigating my mother's safety as she sat in lockdown in her retirement community. Everyone has their stories, and mine were not anywhere near the worst problems going on at that time, nor were they nothing. I sat on Zoom 12 to 14 hours per day, learned about PPP loans, worked to keep my team calm, managed client by client to help each understand who could continue with their engagements, who needed to pause, and who needed to discontinue. When I was not working, I was making meals for my quarantined college kids (now safely home), sanitizing the house and worrying over my mom and my oldest daughter who was sitting in the grief of the loss of her college senior spring and graduation. During this time I saw a social media post that said, "Today is the 182nd day of March." This seemed about right.

In the book, I call all my interviewees Jacks or Jills. As one Jack I re-interviewed told me, our path that started in 2020 followed the stages of grief for all of us trying to transact in business.

Denial: we were sent home from our offices on a Thursday and thought we would be back on Monday. Some of us had the thought to take all of our stuff, most did not. By Monday, we thought it might be three weeks of shutdown, soon we thought six weeks, then we realized it would perhaps be end of summer. Now almost three years later, we never imagined what the road we are on looked like nor how many twists and turns it would take.

Anger: endless virtual meetings, furloughing staff, revenue loss, fear of sickness and death. What would happen to our families, our businesses, our mental health? When would this be over?

Bargaining: perhaps this isn't so bad? I like wearing comfy clothes every day, Netflix is pretty entertaining, I don't have to commute to work, perhaps I should get a puppy?

Depression: especially as we got into late 2020 and winter set in. Days were shorter, colder, darker. Death tolls hit new records. Restrictions were still in place. We experienced more tragedy via the racial reckoning, civil unrest and further bifurcation of our country. Would we ever feel normal again? What did normal really mean anymore?

And lastly, Acceptance: cautiously, we move on with our lives and try to reconnect with family and friends. In business, many of us have changed our model and our talent. We have adapted to remote work or have worked out a hybrid model. Despite the acceptance aspects, we still somewhat automatically hold our collective breath and wait for the next crisis to happen. Most recently as I write this, one major crisis is gun violence—soaring with heartbreak in every new occurrence.

There are silver linings along the path. For me, I survived COVID twice, gained time with my college kids I never would have had, deepened my meditation and yoga practice and reconnected with family and friends with deeper joy and gratitude. For my company, Noetic, our team banded together and committed to our corporate values more than ever before. I learned how to be a better manager, a better business owner. I learned to separate effort from outcome. I learned the meaning of patience at a whole new level.

We watched science progress at warp speed, got vaccines, inaugurated a new president, mourned innumerable deaths. And business rolled on. Sometimes sputtering, sometimes shuttering doors, sometimes thriving more than ever before—depending on one's industry and specific circumstance. We all adopted and quickly fatigued of the word "pivot." We got scrappy. We stressed. We reflected.

In my reflection, I thought a lot about the senior marketers I engage with and that I have known over many years. Especially early in the shutdown, I grew increasingly alarmed as I witnessed so many of them losing jobs. Quickly it was in the double digits. These were highly talented people and it felt shocking. It started to keep me up at night, so I did two things.

First, I started a community that I called Purposeful Connections to enable senior marketing leaders to be able to find one another and share tips and support. We met on Zoom and shared stories. We met one-on-one to help prepare for interviews or for resumé guidance. I ran this group for two years and watched the remarkable journey of these resilient individuals.

Second, I decided to revisit this book, in the chapters that follow here. By speaking with senior marketers about their journey, I was able to unpack the ingredients that enable them to continue to scale the heights. I talked to them about what was still true, more true and newly true in the world we live in now. I listened to their experiences and have shared their wisdom in the pages that follow. I hope this will provide great guidance for you in your journey to scale the heights, especially knowing that the slope of the hill is steeper than ever. I hope you will see and be inspired by their stories of deep learning, creative problem solving and resilience.

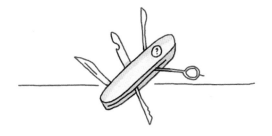

CHAPTER SEVEN

What Is Still True: The Power of Being a Generalist

As discussed in Chapter One, being a generalist has historically gotten a bad rap. People often say "jack of all trades," and it is almost always followed by the criticism: master of none. I am a firm believer, now more than ever, that there is tremendous power in being a generalist with one's greatest superpower within being the ability to learn. Being a lifelong learner is not just about applying oneself, it is about truly loving the process of learning and being willing to put oneself in the seat of trying new things with the inevitable consequence that sometimes you will fail.

Marsha Clark, the author of the excellent book *Embracing Your Power*, explains that we can build our resiliency around making mistakes by leaning into the discomfort of not knowing or not being the expert—safely—with a new skill. She suggests we practice this by choosing a new skill and advises that we choose something we have zero knowledge of nor natural talent for, so that we will be guaranteed to struggle through the learning curve. Marsha says "Pick up a new sport, or a banjo, or a video game—

something where you will get to feel complete frustration, yet you commit to stick with it anyway. Not because you want to be the best (because that will be what your inner critic will start yammering about)…but because you want to learn how to live with and work through mistakes. Lots of them! To build resilience, YOU MUST MAKE MISTAKES! There is no shortcut. Resilience is a capacity you build over time."

One of my most fulfilling learning experiences in 2020 was the Paycheck Protection Program loan program (PPP loans). In my then 19 years as a business owner, I had never borrowed money to run my business, not from investors nor from the government. I was a true novice in this regard, but as I came to understand our situation and how difficult it would be to determine our near future, I became a quick and avid student of the PPP and the process. I researched online, spoke with my banker, tapped into the US Chamber of Commerce and other sources of information. I sat for hours with my head of finance and operations as we methodically completed the application. As uncertain of a time as it was, it was so interesting to understand what might be available and why. As is always true with learning, I got frustrated at times and the yammering in my head was loud. Yet I worked to set aside my fears to get deeply curious—and as I did, I felt the possibilities open up. I talked to other business owners, read the legislation, consulted my banker, and read the fine print until I had it almost memorized.

On April 15, 2020, my company was granted a PPP loan. I do not have to look up this date—I know it by heart and can still picture how the email looked that notified me. Later that day, my banker called to tell me the news firsthand. We were both emotional as we spoke about the plight and passion of small business owners during this extraordinary time. That loan was pivotal in helping my company survive through 2020, and I had to learn an entirely new arena of federal policy and banking procedures to get there.

One Jill put it this way:

There is no playbook for how to manage a global pandemic or if there were it was 100 years old and would not apply in so many ways. The need to bring a nimbleness and being able to meet the challenges and being ready for them as they happen…this may mean being okay with where we are right now and finding the opportunities that are in the set that you have right now. You may not have the right ingredients to do these things, you may have to make the most of what you have. What is good news in this is that often it can be better than what you would have gotten before. This will likely mean different skillsets than you have and you need to grow them and find them. The first step is taking a daily inventory—what are we working with today? what is the skillset? what is the energy level?—and being very keen to read the market. Don't assume that the marketplace is what you thought, continue to ask and pay attention and learn.

Meg Goldthwaite, CMO of The Nature Conservancy

And a Jack who recognizes the connection of high performance and learning:

I recently read a McKinsey study that really resonated with me, as it talked about high performance leaders having consistent discipline in doing postmortems to always look at what you just learned. Develop this muscle so learning is always a part of the equation.

Trip Randall, Former Nike EVP, President of Denon Sound United

Yet another Jack, who pivoted his career from working as a senior marketer in the restaurant industry to opening his own digital marketing agency, directly attributes his success in doing so to his strength as a generalist:

What has helped me the most is having a broad set of skills. I am not deep in anything, but I am really broad and I have a strong ability to adjust and learn. I am learning things now that I never knew I would learn and bringing back things I used to do that I did not realize I would. I believe these days, especially, you need this broad set of skills for your success and for your sanity. I say for your sanity as well because this broad skillset helps me be ready to dig into things I did not know were coming, yet I can do it because I know how to learn well and learn quickly.

Marc Lapides, President of Digital Marketing Partners

Also important is his passion for learning:
I have such a desire to learn about different business models and how they evolve. I have such a wide array of clients…I have e-commerce clients and I had not done e-commerce before. I have a cannabis client and I have never smoked weed. I have a start-up client in sub-Saharan Africa who wanted to sell water there and was not sure how to make money this way. I did not know how to do this either, but I helped him figure it out. With my strong desire to learn and understand how businesses work, I have now written business plans for start-ups and doing this led to their hiring me. For me this was a total accident. I like this part, it is the learning I enjoy the most.

Marc Lapides, President of Digital Marketing Partners

And for this Jill, whose organization was going through bankruptcy due to COVID, she changed the timelines of success and marked each short chapter with learnings before moving on:
For me and for my team, we played a lot with timelines. We focused on smaller arcs for our goals. This really helped us not invest so much work and effort over longer sprints and then have that not work optimally, or even become throwaway.

With everything changing so fast, at any given time we needed to place our bet on what success would look like, the specific needle we were trying to move. Each time we would look at our outcome: did it hit, did it miss? We were continually diligent with the learning—not dwelling on what happened, but on the learning. We celebrated the little wins and displaced frustration with our eye on what we had just learned. This really helped us stay afloat against the backdrop of total chaos.
Laura Smith, Executive Vice President Global Sales, Marketing & Customer Experience at Hertz

What is still true: Noetic 3Cs

You will recall that the Noetic 3Cs are staying connected with your **customer**, minding organization **culture**, and letting **creativity** rule through exploration and play. These days, Jacks and Jills speak about the increased urgency and continual need for customer learning, that culture matters above all else and that creativity has now taken a hit in the remote environment. Let's look at each of the 3Cs.

Staying connected with the customer

Staying close to one's customer has always been important, but in the pandemic it became more difficult to do and even more high stakes *not* to do.

I can tell you firsthand, because my firm specializes in consumer and customer research, that very few companies were investing significantly in staying close to their customers via qualitative and quantitative research through most of 2020. This was partially due to the fact that it felt tone deaf to conduct research on any topic not directly related to COVID-19. This was also true because investing in research was difficult with budgets under greater scrutiny, especially in industries that were suffering significantly from the shutdown. According to Gartner, by the end of 2020, 44 percent of chief marketing officers reported that their budgets had been significantly cut, and Agility PR reported a significant decrease in market research activity based upon overall decreased marketing spend. During this time, many companies did find scrappy, inexpensive ways to stay close to their customers when they could not afford more expensive research studies. For example, Starbucks and L'Oréal more heavily relied on social listening. Apple made greater use of free tools such as Google Analytics. McDonald's experimented using free platforms such as Twitter and Instagram to poll and survey their customers during this period, with many other organizations following their lead.

Starting in 2021, many leaders came to us with new urgency for audience research because they had paused on these efforts. During the pause, they realized their customers had changed so much in such a short period of time that they were unsure what their current needs were. In some cases, they wondered if they were even focused on the right audiences. Indeed, they were right to ask these questions as often their audiences were not the same, nor could they be reached via the same means as before the pandemic. Consumers had begun to rely on digital channels before the pandemic, and this momentum picked up its pace significantly when none of us could move about. McKinsey reported a notable correlation between an increased desire for convenience with the timing of retail operations closing or operating under limited conditions. Services such as curbside pickup and same-day delivery became new staples for many people, and for many these new habits are continuing.

Consumers have grown accustomed to having convenient shopping options and will likely continue counting on them even as pre-pandemic behaviors return, creating a new post-pandemic shopping norm. Look at prom dress shopping, for example. My youngest daughter and her friends would never consider shopping in a store for a dress now, because the inventory is lacking and overall options will be slim. They order multiple options online where retailers offer free, easy return shipping, and use their own bedrooms as their fitting room.

Even though digital shopping has sharply increased, consumers are shopping less overall since 2020. One-third of Americans have reported a decrease in their household income during the crisis, and 40 percent say they are spending more carefully. Indeed, consumers expect to spend less in discretionary categories, such as apparel, vehicles, and travel, while more on essentials such as groceries and household supplies.

In today's environment, Jacks and Jills observe these types of mindset and behavioral shifts and predict it will continue to evolve more quickly than in the Before Times, making it essential to study consumers and stay close at all times. They also emphasize the need to provide as much authentic value as possible, as customers care more deeply about corporation's choices and actions in environmental and social decisions.

Marketers need to start with the consumer—that has not changed and is even more imperative because so much change is happening and you could be acting on insights that may have already expired. Listen to those insights and make sure you are useful in consumers' lives. There is no room now for things that are not useful. When I say useful, it may perhaps be an app that brings you puffy little snowball puppies because they make you happy—it does not have to be true utility but it is useful in some way. Brands have an obligation to play a role in peoples' lives and there is more responsibility than there ever was. Start with their journey, meet them where they are—peoples' hard drives are filling up. We think of young people as having a voracious appetite but they too are looking for usefulness.

Trip Randall, Former Nike EVP, current President of Denon Sound United

One of the most important things now is to strive to understand your customer. Over time you may feel you have a good grasp on who they are, listening to round out the edges in the old world. Today this may be a complete revisiting. So much of the deck of cards got thrown up in the air, so it may require a wholesale new set of considerations of what is important to these people and also, who are these people?! We are no longer the herd—it has morphed or even mutated, and now we need a new understanding of what those herds are—and this is what we do as marketers.

Gordon Montgomery, Vice President, Marketing and Communications at Caravel Autism Health

Consumers' perceptions and behaviors have changed dramatically and very quickly. At the end of the day all things in marketing are driven by consumer perceptions and behaviors, and I have never seen them change so rapidly.

We all must keep our finger on the pulse of it continually.
The need for this level of agility will not go away.

Cathy Davis, former Chief Marketing
Officer of Feeding America

I think research has become ever more important in this
market. We have done more research of our alumni base,
our students. We have redone our journey mapping
because so much has changed. I also think people have
become more curious - perhaps due to the social unrest.
Internally we really want and need to understand where
people are getting their beliefs and attitudes. We are deeply
curious about what the differentiations are in the world
and how does it affect our brand and each of us.

Jan Slater, Chief Marketing Officer at Gies
College of Business, University of Illinois

From a consumer lens, fandom and loyalty and brand are 5x
more important than they were even a couple of years ago
because people have slowed down and had the moment to
see what is really out there - especially in the entertainment
world. So they are able to make very clear choices. You need
to continue to know show that you know who your consumer
is. It is even more important now because you have to
understand how they have changed; their habits have changed,
their priorities have changed. We are on a change path and so
are our consumers. We need to continually stay on top of it.

Lara Richardson, Chief Marketing Officer,
Crown Media Family Networks

We really need more focus than ever on our consumers.
There is significant change here, but there is nostalgia too...
for the before times. For example, grocery shopping will

not go back to what it was. There will be people who will
do it online, but there are people who love to go there. It is
essential to understand these segments and think about
the implications versus how the model used to be. It is a
new path. pay close attention to new attitudes, behaviors,
preferences because these have changed drastically. Now is
the time to do market research. There is a great resurgence of
demand for market research and it is essential that we do it.

Sumedha Mandpe, AVP Retention
Marketing, Nationwide Financial

Minding your organizational culture

At the beginning of the shutdown, most of the marketing leaders I spoke with leaned in to communicating more often and more candidly with their teams. They sought to understand as much as possible, what each person was dealing with and how to best support them. They looked at the culture of their organization: how it was shifting, how it was showing up and what could they do to strengthen it, with the feeling that, if they did not focus on strengthening people's connection to each other and the organization, these ties would inevitably weaken.

I pursued this path in my company, as well, especially as it related to frequent and candid communication, and leaned into our values. It was amazing to me that at each and every difficult moment, I could find guidance in what to do somewhere within our values. For example, one of our core values is Help and Kindness First. This means looking for proactive ways to help people around us: each other, our clients, our friends. When we do this, we never know what specific positive result we will achieve, yet time and again it yields amazing things. This can be as small as making someone smile who is having a difficult day, as big as helping someone find a new job, and anything in between. Spending time on this deepens our cultural commitment and attracts positive energy and a sense of community.

noetic *note*

At Noetic, when we are hired to help an organization reimagine or refine the audience and/or their brand, we first ask leadership to tell us about their overall organizational Purpose, Vision, Mission and Values. While at times these elements do exist, leaders usually share that they are just words on their website. We start from where they are and help them determine whether the ideas are right, what needs to be adjusted and then work through how these can be authentically activated within the organization. Most often we do this in what we call co-creation workshops, where leaders from various functions come together to create or re-create these elements in community. They determine what actions they will commit to and ask all leaders to live these in their day-to-day.

I think sometimes when the pieces of what we come to know fall apart, we need to ask ourselves, what can we harken back to? To me the biggest thing to reground in is being true to our values. We may trip over the specific words or approaches but can we convey in some way what we do, the values we stand for. It is also important as we do this to have patience with each other and with ourselves. That we all try to lead with good intention. If we can be humble, self-effacing and honest —this is not perfect, but by following best logic we can do our best yet stay open to feedback. Just be purposeful and well intended, and acknowledge the imperfections.

Gordon Montgomery, Vice President, Marketing and Communications at Caravel Autism Health

During any crisis, people are stressed, which creates stress to the culture. This dynamic pulls us away from each other, rather than naturally bringing us together. Working remotely, needing to isolate, feeling provoked and heartbroken about racial inequities and civil unrest, all stoke our fear and pull us inward. Like a riptide in a tumultuous sea, we find ourselves swirling alone and further away from the very thing that can help us surface—coming together. As the New York Times put it, "Fear is the primary driver of this crisis. Public companies live in morbid fear of being outflanked by competitors, failing to meet their quarterly targets and watching helplessly as their stocks are pummeled by impatient investors. Leaders and managers live in fear of not delivering their numbers and losing their jobs, so they look constantly for ways to cut expenses—and head counts—which puts ever more pressure on their employees to do more with fewer resources. It's a vicious, accelerating cycle that serves no one well."

As we find ourselves in the vortex of this cycle, tending to our culture is the most valuable lever we have—second only to tending to ourselves (which I will speak about in the next chapter.) The numbers bear this out: a Columbia University study shows that the likelihood of job turnover at an organization with strong company culture is a mere 13.9 percent, whereas the probability of job turnover in weak company cultures is 48.4 percent. I recently spoke with a Jill who is new in an organization, and working 100% remote. When I asked her about the culture, she paused for a long moment, then said, "I don't think there is any culture here. I literally cannot get a beat on it. We are new, everyone has their heads down working, I don't know anyone at all. I will give it time to see if I am wrong, but if I am not, I will not stay."

How did we stay together? We were in the process of building out a new value statement in the college. We had taken our old vision, mission and values and felt it did not fit us anymore. So we built a purpose statement and made strategic priorities. We really started talking about values...I think we thought about them more carefully because of the time we were in. We had some values we all believed in that became really powerful to help us get through. For example, one is called "common humanity" - it is about how you treat people, the kind of respect you show, that we need to be authentic in who we are and what we do.

Jan Slater, Chief Marketing Officer at Gies College of Business, University of Illinois

Relationships and culture are the basis of all. We are all humans, and we often give lip service to empathy, but it is culture that can really make empathy come to life. When the rubber meets the road, are you truly an empathetic leader? You cannot say we need results at all costs and out of other side of your mouth say, please do self care. It goes back to relationships. If you don't trust people, if you do not know how to motivate people...your culture will erode in this ever challenging environment.

Sumedha Mandpe, AVP Retention Marketing, Nationwide Financial

In Marketing and Communications, we often just think about it from an external standpoint. Internal communication is so important. With these big bumps in the road, how are we helping people navigate? As you strengthen your culture, you need to recognize you have different audiences. Equally challenging have been the political implications of this period and this has become more complex especially

when working across geographies. For example, YOU
have to wear a mask -- but YOU do not. How do you unite
people yet speak with a different voice when it is needed?

**Gordon Montgomery, Vice President, Marketing
and Communications at Caravel Autism Health**

And as you have likely seen, in many cases leaders and team members are making significant changes when the culture and environment end up not feeling a fit for what matters most to them now. One Jill explained it this way:

There are things that are important to me now that I would
not even have known a year ago. I attended the most open,
transparent townhall just yesterday. There was such a
connection amongst everyone. This is a smaller organization
(than my previous) with a very values-based culture. The
values are empathy, trust, love. I thought it was super weird for
it to be about love! But people love the brand and our customers
do also. This is what has the deep meaning for me now.
connection amongst everyone. This is a smaller organization
(than my previous) with a very values-based culture. The
values are empathy, trust, love. I thought it was super weird for
it to be about love! But people love the brand and our customers
do also. This is what has the deep meaning for me now.

Barb Goose, Chief Marketing Officer at Rocket Software

Letting Creativity Rule

Creativity and collaboration—which so often go hand in hand—have become a great debate starting in 2020. Many believe remote working, shutdowns of creative venues and overall stress are key contributors to a decline in collaboration and creativity. Several Jacks and Jills worry about the dynamic and encourage leaders to find ways to enhance these aspects to ensure innovation and fresh thinking can still thrive.

I have always appreciated the saying, "if you want to go fast go alone, if you want to go far, go together." When we are all in different places, we are all independently working and we can do things quicker in many ways but we cannot go as far because we are not under the same strategy emotionally, and physically…and this is basically our situation in this remote world. Working this way pales in comparison to sitting in a room and going through something. Many people may say it is not a problem. I am saying, this is a problem.

Derek Koenig, Chief Marketing Officer/
Head of Creative, Buffalo Groupe

What did not work: the stuff that we would do to collaborate in the office…white boarding, rounds of brainstorming, challenging and building on ideas…this experience was missing and continues to be a challenge. I was able to bring in my direct reports a few times at a social distance but there were lots of sensitivities to some people being immune compromised and I had to respect this.

AK Singh, Associate Principal, ZS

While several studies show face to face gatherings produce more ideas and more inventive ones, the market trends and research show it is not all bleak. For example, a national study revealed more than half of Americans have picked-up a new creative pastime, or revisited an old one, since the arrival of COVID-19, with 98 percent of those that have taken up a new hobby continuing to practice at least once per week. Another study by a Northwestern Kellogg professor cites extensive research proving "necessity breeds invention" is a ruling force and creative output increases in restrictive circumstances.

While the debate will likely continue, our Jacks and Jills are clear that practicing collaboration and leaning into creativity require more effort in today's environment. They recommend learning new virtual tools and being particularly thoughtful about when to assemble together in real life.

What is still true: Noetic 4Ps

As you read earlier, hiring great data **p**eople, **p**reparing well, committing to strong **p**erformance metrics and **p**racticing new skills were important key aspects for Jacks and Jills in the Before Times, and are still critical today.

From my new discussion with senior marketers these days, **practicing new skills** has moved to the top of this list, as day-to-day business dynamics continue to shift and skillset needs shift with them. Reorganizations inside businesses, people seeking new jobs (unintentionally or by choice), and failing industries exponentiate this need. Early on in the pandemic as we watched our consumer research services lack demand, we simultaneously observed our training and coaching services pick up volume. This was curious to me at first, because in the Before Times we would often see training and coaching as vulnerable budget items when financial times got tough. Here we were in tough times, yet enlightened leaders understood the importance of improving the skills and resilience of their marketers and leaders.

To effectively handle the level of crisis and the speed of it all that was coming at us, we needed clear objectives, we needed to know the boundaries, and we needed to be able to relocate people into factions where we needed them. We needed agility and flexibility with each and every person. And this need for agility is not going away.

Cathy Davis, former Chief Marketing Officer of Feeding America

*In the hierarchy of needs we cannot be tone deaf. Everything
is temporary. Nothing is formulaic. If you don't accept
that and you are not prepared every day to work with
what you have, there is so much that can go wrong. You
must practice new ways of thinking, learn new skills as
you need them, try new things and let go of old ways.*

**Meg Goldthwaite, Chief Marketing Officer
of The Nature Conservancy**

*We are not islands. We solved problems together. We learned
together. I tell this to my team: it is really easy to get stuck
in: yes or no...this way or that way. what we really need is to
think in nonbinary problem solving. This is a different way of
thinking and a new skill. You as one person cannot possibly
have all those answers yourself. Show your vulnerability
with your team to show you don't have answers and tap
them, or go to your peers as your thought partners.*

**Jan Slater, Chief Marketing Officer at Gies
College of Business, University of Illinois**

As the CMO of Waze, Erin Clift, explained it, "Marketers
have had to quickly pivot to understand rapidly changing market
landscapes, consumer behavior and business challenges. And
we've all had to find new ways to work with different parts of our
organizations, as well as external partners, to collaborate, create
and execute work." Clift is not alone in her position with this belief:
Deloitte reports that over 40 percent of all CMOs nationally believe
their teams need more training. As 2020 rolled into 2021 and we
began to experience the Great Resignation, talent development has
risen to the top of the agenda for most C-suite executives.

As a place to start the Noetic Art & Science Assessment
provides strong insight on individual strengths and opportunities

as it relates to the core skills marketers need to scale the heights. You can take this quiz yourself from this book, or access it online on our website (www.noeticconsultants.com). You can have your team take it as well in order to determine the collective needs you have for skilling up.

CHAPTER EIGHT

What Is More True: Put Your Mask on First

Like all of us, senior marketers are people first and struggled first, as people. This was particularly true for those who found themselves out of work. While these folks were not alone—almost 10 percent of all marketing positions were eliminated during the shutdown, with almost 30 percent of these at the senior level—it was nonetheless a shock to the system of high achieving Jacks and Jills. They vulnerably shared their struggle to adjust, the uncomfortable feelings of decompressing and ultimately the value of doing nothing. After years—for some decades—of working at high performance every day, they felt distinctly uncomfortable *not* working. Yet when they finally embraced this new situation, they learned the strong value and insight from focusing on *being* versus doing, and they leaned in to giving themselves this space.

I have been enjoying not being in the grind. It took awhile to shed it—and I did this by doing nothing. As an accomplished marketer, I am always looking for a new perspective, I am always striving to be on my A game. Always striving, always selling—to your boss, to other internal people. The hardest sell is the pre- consumer sell, where you need to get key people on board internally. As a senior marketer you are always trying to get the new thinking out there. I believe every executive lives off of the adrenaline of this fight—fighting to be heard, to see the value of the idea. So I needed to step back from all of this and have space. Uncomfortable but very valuable.

Ken Dice, former Global Vice President, Nike

I did a lot of self-reflection and took a break in a way I never have before. As I was leaving the pandemic hit, so firstly it was acceptance of what was happening. The absence of choice really helps you focus and lean in to where you are! Perhaps I would have gotten into conferences and classes to push for an evolution, make the most of this sabbatical... instead I found myself leaning into my personal life in a way that I never had before—second only to maternity leaves and one stint in 2007 when I transitioned from for profit to nonprofit...but even those experiences were not really "take a minute." This time I really gave myself permission to be the person in my family that was needed at that time...for my adult children as they transitioned to remote school, managing my house as my husband was working in ED tech—which was really taking off then. Really just being—not a choice I would have made, yet the world made it for me.

Meg Goldthwaite, Chief Marketing Officer of The Nature Conservancy

My company went through major change in 2020, and by spring of 2021 it was time for me to move on. The job was not what I wanted anymore though I highly regarded them and still do today.

*It was really humbling to stop working. It was a mutual decision
for me to leave. But I love working! It was hard to be without
a job. My identity is very connected to the job and the people
I am with. I am so motivated by the team. Suddenly not being
surrounded by a team was just strange. And then I needed to
think about, what am I really good at? What do I really want?*

*I talked to many companies, and sometimes I did not get
chosen where I thought I would. I learned a lot about myself.
It was the first time in my career that I could really reflect and
say, what do I want to do? I thought about what marketing
really meant and what I wanted it to mean for me.*

Barb Goose, Chief Marketing Officer at Rocket Software

This past fall I had the incredible opportunity to visit Sedona,
Arizona. I was even more fortunate to be able to connect with a
friend of a friend who has been a guide at Sedona for over 20 years.
Dennis took an entire day to show us the best of Sedona, including
leading me in a life-changing guided meditation as the sun set. My
level of gratitude was so intense at the end of this experience that I
literally sputtered to him, "I don't know how to thank you and I feel
really uncomfortable about it."

Given the sage he is, Dennis laughed and said, "Well, it would
be interesting to unpack why that is so." Then he told me that his
greatest thanks would be if I would consider more being than
doing in my life.

"So just *be* more…like, doing…whatever? Or doing nothing?"

"Yes," he said, "you will really have to work hard at it."

And these Jacks and Jills did just that. (I, alas, am a work in
progress in this regard.) As they worked to shift gears, establish
new focus and thrive in their new situations, they shared with me
the tools that they used. Some tools were tried and true and they

dug in deeper with them. Others were new or newly rediscovered. Always getting back up and dusting themselves off, they shared this expanded toolbox of ways that they have worked to keep themselves and when they had them, their teams—grounded, connected and psychologically healthy.

Critical items in this expanded toolbox include exercise, meditation, walks, staying connecting with others, having a designated workspace, adjusting their work schedule and focusing on the very next task as a way of combatting overwhelm.

While I have been an almost daily exerciser for many years now, I had the lucky opportunity to buy a Peloton just before the shutdown. This was not in the least that I saw it coming. Rather, it was that my youngest daughter and I had been spending a lot of time taking spin classes and we thought a Peloton would give us a more frequent opportunity to do this with consistency. I am eternally grateful that from the start of the shutdown I had that bike to work out my anxieties on the pedals each day.

A morning workout was and still is the most important thing. Cycling, and walks. These are critical for me. I also needed time to think and to de-stress.

Cathy Davis, former Chief Marketing Officer of Feeding America

In addition to exercise, I believe it is also super important to keep my network going. I made connections at least once per week and even increased it since it was easier to do more of this in virtual. Connecting with people has always been an important part of my success, and by continuing to make it a priority it has led to all sorts of things in the last couple of years—including new business we brought in. It was hard to commit to this—there was such a strong pull to cocoon and isolate. I felt this and saw it in others. Many times I saw that people were happy afterward but were a bit resistant to make the effort to get together, even virtually.

Pat Lafferty, Chief Operations Officer,
Acceleration Community of Companies

As part of taking care of myself I worked on caring for my career: self assessments, coaching, going to the PC group. The amount of stress was at a whole different level and it was work related. I needed a way to connect with myself and others. Staying committed to connecting with others was tremendous and it also connected me with people I never would have connected with otherwise.

Sumedha Mandpe, AVP Retention
Marketing, Nationwide Financial

I asked myself each day, "Did we move forward?" If I felt we did, I deemed it a good day. I also moved to a time block schedule. Time management was the hardest—I had to shift everything I knew, had to think about how I spend my time, think really differently about how I do everything and when I do it. At first I tried to do traditional office hours in this new world...but now it is a block plan. I have people all over the country, colleagues overseas. So I intersperse with personal things, and break up time differently.

Trip Randall, Former Nike EVP, current
President of Denon at Sound United

The most important was getting okay with being where I am right now. I had already developed a habit of meditating every day, so this was easy to do and keep doing. But now my whole routine was tossed in the air so I had to make sure that I brought the discipline of my meditation to the rest of my day. Working at purely being, right there, in that moment, and the acceptance that yes, I am having anxiety surges and saying okay, that is interesting, this is what this feels like. I needed to create routine and structure. And also have small goals. No matter how small, make my goal and hit it and know I got a win for the day. This was very important for management of anxiety. Fitness was also a big part. I am a wanderer, I want to be out...fitness gave me a moment to myself when there were so many people in my house (with my older kids home). I had become such a caretaker, this helped me remember me as me.

Meg Goldthwaite, CMO of The Nature Conservancy

Personally, the situation we found ourselves in really made me rethink things. It made me really thoughtful about self care. Before that time I would meditate, eat healthy and exercise, but I took it for granted. When the pandemic started it was really hard and I saw myself go downhill. When I saw so many things being taken away from me and all of us, I got stressed and started binge eating...and that is not me. This helped me know I needed to be extremely thoughtful for myself and also for my family and all those around me. So I got very intentional about 45 minutes of running, 15 minutes of walking in the Botanical Gardens when weather permitted, in time that I boxed and protected to do this.

**Sumedha Mandpe, Director, Digital &
Growth Marketing, Grail Inc.**

My morning routine with exercise was critical, this keeps me grounded and centered. I could not be with others playing tennis, but I found other ways to connect with people, mostly in my backyard. I start my day working on something with more meaning. This is critical. I need to spend at least an hour each morning working on something meaningful that is attached to my top three priorities...

*then I know and will always have the satisfaction at the
end of the day that I accomplished something meaningful
against my top three, no matter what else the day holds.*

AK Singh, Associate Principal, ZS

*Finding myself an office was key for me. It was so easy to just
get up, work, go to bed. But this was not a good way to live.
Before I had a separate office, my office was where we hung
out at night also—so there was no boundary. Now I have clear
separation of work and home. I know a lot of people have
lost this. It is now very easy for me to separate and this was
important because it brought a sense of normal and prevented
burnout. When everything was at home, the cocoon allowed me
to do anything I wanted for as long as I wanted, but it was not
necessarily good for me. Ultimately I got the office because my
wife kicked me out during the work day, but I was good with it!*

Mark Lapides, President of Digital Marketing Partners

*In my personal life, I gave myself a new kind of routine.
It was so hard in my home, I would see all the things that
needed to be done. I needed discipline to do home things
outside of the work hours to reduce the powerlessness
that I felt. I always got up to exercise, so I still did that. I
re-established a full routine—my dog went to daycare
before the shut down, so I kept taking him. At one point
Uber Eats got out of control so we had to adjust this!*

Barb Goose, Chief Marketing Officer at Rocket Software

*I learned at a whole new level, the importance of focusing
on the very next thing that needs to get done. If a day gets
totally off track, I will ask myself if I did the best I can?
Sometimes I have to be honest that I avoided a task because
it was unpleasant when it really was the thing I needed to*

do. I know there will be things that pull at me...it helps me
focus and I find it satisfying to accomplish against my list.

Trip Randall, Former Nike EVP, current
President of Denon Sound United

I worked harder during COVID and I think everyone
did. At first I worked so much on screen but then the
sheer exhaustion and screen fatigue hit hard. I advocate
for mental health, for establishing boundaries. You
can do a great job and not work 24/7. This must be a
focus and a goal or the work can overtake you.

Barb Goose, Chief Marketing Officer at Rocket Software

For their teams, leaders committed to more frequent and continual communication, with different formats and overtly making time for nonwork conversation. Many Jacks and Jills spoke of an increased frequency to one-on-one meetings, with the national average jumping 43 percent for this format alone. And as we all know, most all of these communications were now happening in virtual platforms. Statista reported that Zoom video use was up to 300 million daily meetings worldwide by as early as April 2020—less than a month into the shutdown. They also cited that one in three companies worldwide adopted some form of video and/or live chat channels during this time, with an average of 3.5 new channels adopted per company.

Leaders are wise to spend time and resources in this area, as *Harvard Business Review* notes that increased communication, safe channels for giving feedback and helping workers work effectively from home were three of the biggest factors for employee satisfaction since 2020. Adopting these new practices is no silver bullet, however. Many leaders observed over time that spontaneous personal connections and team collaborations did not happen without overt effort to create them. And with an overload of virtual, they observed team members becoming transactional and at times more passive or distracted.

noetic *note*

During the last three years at Noetic, we have seen our executive coaching of marketing leaders completely take off. This was a service that organically grew from our training practice and from our informal guidance that we have provided to marketers for years. As marketing executives work to stand up new functions, take on new positions, address burnout and lead their teams effectively, they increasingly benefit from having a confidential resource that helps them think through their own purpose, values and leadership priorities. We are also able to help them skill up where needed when they come into new positions that require different art or science skills. One of the biggest areas of focus in coaching these days is how these leaders communicate in order to be most effective in their roles.

Instead of doing one-on-ones with my team like I had always done, I stopped them and started a full direct reports meeting three times per week. It was good for each department head to hear what was going on with the others even if this information was not overtly relevant to them. After awhile people started to see and feel more connected, and we started getting out of our siloes more. I told people I could do one-on-ones if they needed it on ad hoc basis, but this new format really helped people as individuals and as a team.

**Lara Richardson, Chief Marketing Officer,
Crown Media Family Networks**

We went to a weekly staff meeting at 9 a.m. on Monday mornings. A lot of this time was spent on "Here is what I know, here is what is happening." A lot of it was about work, but this also gave us the opportunity of looking at what we needed help with and what we needed to talk about. I also did regular check ups with everyone as often as possible. Across a two week time span I would get one to one with each staff member. We were using Microsoft Teams in January of 2020, just before shutdown. We really embraced this and set up various kinds of channels. We had a general channel where people started saying when they had to step away. We made a fun, light note channel for birthdays and other celebrations. We made a "finished work" channel, where anytime a job got done, this was the place to see the work that was going out into the world. The real jewel of this was that things were able to be translated to other areas, we got true cross fertilization. We kept it and still keep it authentic and transparent—not a place to complain.

Jan Slater, Chief Marketing Officer at Gies College of Business, University of Illinois

To stay connected as a team, we did two things: each day I met with six people for 30 minutes and talked about anything but work. We did this as skip level, so it was anyone except my direct reports. I called it "staying connected." It was purely a chance for people to talk and know each other. Second, I used to do monthly stand up get togethers. But during this time we realized we needed shorter, more frequent meetings. So I started biweekly 30 minute meetings where I would do the introduction and then people would present what they were doing, would show their progress, their hard work and their results.

Barb Goose, Chief Marketing Officer at Rocket Software

I am a connected leader, so I really made a point to try to bring some humanity to Zoom. We had more fun in Zoom than we did in live—everyone would come, remembering to laugh before we got down to the work, always taking time to celebrate wins, and check in on each other because people would not raise hands if they were struggling—they would just go dark. As someone who prides himself on knowing his teams, I learned way more making sure we had each others' backs and checking in on each other than I ever had at any other time. We should be doing this anyway—a global pandemic should not be required to care deeply at a human level and show that caring regularly. We carry this with us the same as how we all now fully carry the belief that we should all wear comfy shoes all the time.

Trip Randall, Former Nike EVP, President of Denon Sound United

When I did one-to-one meetings with peers, I did them on the phone not on video, in order to give people a break from always being on camera. I used this and encouraged others to use it as an opportunity to walk and move. This was good for me and for my team members.

After we got through the biggest part of the crisis, we needed to make sure that people took their boundaries back: creating more flexibility, recognizing the mental health implications, letting people take a day when they needed. We needed a certain informality and I had to set that tone so they would know it was okay, this was the new normal (and it was kind of lovely in a lot of ways.) I had to give people the permission to do what they needed to do.

Cathy Davis, former Chief Marketing Officer of Feeding America

I have tried to stay in personal contact as much as possible. During this time, I have actually gone to the office more. I find great value in this, it creates opportunity and connections. It provides support to myself and to others. There are so many interstitial moments lost with virtual—the walks between meetings, the body language, the overall socialization... perhaps this is less so for the older set who have many relationships but for young people this is the biggest loss.

Gordon Montgomery, Vice President, Marketing and Communications at Caravel Autism Health

Something I instituted for my team—for meetings, I set aside five to ten minutes for chitchat. This did not strike me as so big of a thing immediately. Over time, I saw that this dramatically shifts our connection with our fellow workers. Without this, we were totally transactional.

AK Singh, Associate Principal, ZS

Jacks and Jills running marketing in organizations where the crisis was hitting particularly hard tended to practice the most intense efforts in communication and had the highest frequency. Those in bankruptcy, in healthcare, in hospitality or other industries where the Before Times looked nothing like COVID times. The more their teams were working without a playbook, the more they felt the need and saw the value of speaking continually and candidly, with a focus on making meaning where they could.

noetic *note*

Our team is certified in DiSC® training to help leaders and teams understand their personal working style and preferences, and that of their teams. When leaders learn their styles, they come to better understand why they are energized by some activities or interactions while fatigued by others. They learn how to stretch into other styles to improve communication, collaboration and to more constructively handle conflict. These skills and behaviors are even more important today as we work in remote or hybrid environments, where it becomes harder to connect informally and to grasp emotional cues. Our virtual or live work sessions help teams unlock this understanding and practice their stretching together.

As a senior manager, your job is to create culture and instill the behavior of how you want your team to do the work. It is very hard to do this these days, but this is the job. I see many managers go it alone and you have to go together. Lift people up and ferret it out if you have bullies. These can be harder to identify in remote.

Derek Koenig, Chief Marketing Officer/ Head of Creative, Buffalo Groupe

I quickly moved to an all-hands global huddle meeting where we literally had every single person at the company involved in almost in every discussion. We were in crisis, we did not have time to cascade messages from the senior level to the more junior. Everyone was in the same boat and needed to be. We were almost obsessive about it. We would reset every Monday: what needs to happen this week? This rhythm and drumbeat gave us the fly wheel effect and got us out of the hierarchy of translating messages. We included open Q&A, we kept it very dynamic and fast moving. We continue with this in Teams and everyone knows it is active; the conversation is always happening. It took a bit of time to get people to be willing to speak up. Once they saw that they were supported even when they gave difficult feedback or asked pointed questions. People have learned and grown from it and now it is expected.

Laura Smith, Executive Vice President Global Sales, Marketing & Customer Experience at Hertz

They were also honest about the things they tried that *did not work.*

It was hard for people to take their boundaries back after we got through the initial crisis mode. This is very necessary but not everyone could do it. People want control or a feeling of control. I think this is why people are doing side hustles as it feels like more control of own destiny. And people who are participating in the Great Resignation—they are seeking a different destiny.

Cathy Davis, former Chief Marketing Officer of Feeding America

Being in a health system, the pandemic had a whole different level of impact. We were headed in one direction before the pandemic. Then for a behemoth to make a turn to a new direction...it was chaotic to do it, it affected everyone, and it was very difficult to get people to understand and do it. How do you communicate? Every day a new change was happening. There was no playbook and people were used to a playbook. Everyone got tossed in the air. We tried to help people embrace change and move at lightning speed. And not everyone could do it. Some people walked out. We tried to communicate a ton, yet it never seemed enough. There were times I believe we were very reactionary. And failure was not an option—so this created fear and pressure.

Sumedha Mandpe, AVP Retention Marketing, Nationwide Financial

I have not solved this, but we have stopped happy hour Zooms. This evolved to feeling it was forcing people to spend more time on Zoom. I do not really have a true solve for this yet. I am meeting my team in a park coming up. *I have been pushing for this in person. I am not sure if, when the time comes, it will feel right. Will we be in a surge, will people feel comfortable, is it safe enough? We are riding the wave of where we are in the process.*

Lara Richardson, Chief Marketing Officer, Crown Media Family Networks

CHAPTER NINE

What Is Newly True: In Crisis, Start with Art, Follow with Science

As leaders saw the changes happening, and the speed at which they were shifting, they understood the imperative to act quickly and move on gut instinct. They spoke at length about using their emotions to guide their actions and feeling their way to solutions and innovations. This is consistent with what we also saw in organizations making large changes out of necessity, including liquor companies manufacturing antibacterial lotions from spirits, airlines carrying freight instead of passengers, and the vast majority of companies enlisting work from home practices unless physical presence was needed to get the job done.

This type of actioning is all **Art**, and in crisis, leaders consistently attest that being artful is the way to take action. By artful, they mean the aspects that are available in the Art toolbox, such as leveraging gut instinct, using imagination, generating ideas and storytelling. They lead with art skills and behaviors in these situations because it is the only practical way; there is literally no time to gather data before making decisions when the decisions must be made so quickly. Yet this is not the only reason that Art is the lead horse in crisis. When we experience any form of feeling unsafe, the amygdala, an organ in the middle of our brains, kicks into gear. The amygdala alerts our nervous system, which sets our body's fear response into motion. At this point stress hormones like cortisol and adrenaline are released, and we might feel our heart rate increase, our tummy flip, our head pound. This type of emotional reaction hinders our ability to use our rational reasoning, which comes from a different part of our brains. Rather than fight or ignore this reality, Jacks and Jills ride this wave toward a calmer current by acknowledging the emotions and empathetically addressing them. They do this with honesty, continual communication and by meeting people where they are.

With art as the lead horse, Jacks and Jills were careful to emphasize that science is more important than ever to validate and further direct, yet it often needs to come after key actions have been taken to check and verify, then help change course as necessary. In particular these days they see more risk to not doing this type of homework in an increasing tech driven marketing world.

Grounding in data always comes back to time with customers, thinking ahead of the trends, and paying attention to micro trends that will have implication and impact within the category in which you exist. For example, how will people us transportation in different geographies? What will the barriers be? It is critical to have a beat on research—making sure there is not something else happening that we are not aware of. All the metrics must help inform. Then we can be sure the team hits the right strategic initiative.

Laura Smith, Executive Vice President Global Sales, Marketing & Customer Experience at Hertz

It is imperative that we continue to pay attention to the things that define our core. We are supposed to be the voice of the consumer and operate with empathy. The behavior changes and preferences have gotten very accelerated. In healthcare, before the pandemic, 30 percent of the population was willing to receive virtual care. Now this is above 70 percent. We must pay attention because the old playbook is outdated. We must analyze and adjust our messaging or it will be obsolete.

Data and tech have always been around, yet the fundamentals of the toolkit have continued to evolve. But what I realize, and I believe we all need to realize in business not just marketing, is that everyone is in the data and tech business now. I saw this happening around me and I thought, there will only be two kinds of leaders—either you will be a leader who will embrace data and tech with both arms, and will make sure you know how to use these tools to do your job better, or you will be reluctant, keep them at arm's length or keep them in a silo. This will define what kind of fulfillment you will feel in the work you do. If you embrace data and technology, you can solve meaningful problems that can have impact. Let's face it, unless you understand the trends surrounding us and having a finer appreciation for who to partner with, to work together in an integrated way, it will not be as satisfying and you will be ill-informed.

AK Singh, Associate Principal, ZS

The Noetic Art & Science assessment can give you an objective understanding of your appetite and acumen for the science side of things, with practical suggestions that follow on how to strengthen these muscles if needed.

What is *newly* true: don't let strategy get in the way of action

With a full blend of art and science, Jacks and Jills spoke of the imperative of focusing on what needs to be done *right now.* This doesn't mean to sacrifice strategy nor one's gut instinct, but rather to blend the two to focus on the very next step up the hill.

The thing I do every day is I write down a list of what has to get done the next day and try to deliver on this as much as possible—line up my calendar and all my tasks to it. Nothing has helped me more than this in my current job.

Trip Randall, Former Nike EVP, President of Denon Sound United

As far as the team, I have been having them work on "what is in front of me today?" It sounds cliche but one day at a time is really valuable. What do you have control over and what don't you have control over? For example, everyone is worried about the return to office. This is not in your power, so don't focus on it. Celebrate the good, don't look too far forward or too far back.

Lara Richardson, Chief Marketing Officer, Crown Media Family Networks

If this extraordinary time has proved anything, it is that we have to be more agile than ever before. My mom used to joke, "best laid plans—what is the good of those?" In my ad agency, we were always planning. I am a natural strategist and I am all for strategy, but you have to be ready to adjust and replan and move quickly. You have to be ready to change course when needed. You have to be willing to make hard decisions and you may need to be quicker than you want to and you may be making more mistakes. Your best mental plan is to know and accept that this will happen.

Jan Slater, Chief Marketing Officer at Gies College of Business, University of Illinois

In my own journey, I have employed a *Miracle Mornings* practice developed by Hal Elrod that focuses me on the here and now and enables me to make a specific plan of approach for each day. While I had been doing some of the practices this author suggests, the addition of 10 minutes of silence and writing down affirmations and visualizations each day enables me to ground myself in the now and what I want to get done on this particular day. Perhaps most importantly, 10 minutes of silence that I can count on each morning gives me a feeling of collecting myself that powerfully balances me and staves off the overwhelm of the volume of work, the uncertainty and the desire to know more of what the future will look like.

Another helpful resource I discovered during COVID was *Positive Intelligence*, a book, app and methodology created by Shirzad Chamine that teaches leaders how to recognize and thereby weaken the negative voices in our heads—what Shirzad calls "our Saboteurs." I was particularly fortunate that my Vistage coach Ed Robinson gifted me this program at the beginning of January 2021, which happened to be the moment when I got COVID. As you will recall, this was before vaccinations were available, and I got quite sick. Having a methodology that I could learn and practice (listening to the app as I lay with my eyes closed) was exactly the lifeline I needed at that moment as I could not know how long I would be sick, nor how bad things would get. I needed to stay grounded in the very moment and go to the next moment, let go of having any longer or broader plans. I spent 14 days living in this moment to moment reality and it was the best practice of mindfulness I have ever experienced. To be clear, I am not saying I enjoyed having COVID. Indeed, I was suffering greatly. But letting go of having a strategy and simply actioning to the very next moment enabled me to heal in the only way that could happen.

Lastly, I started a very simple practice in 2020 that I use almost every day to ensure I am taking the right action, right now. I look at my task list (which is very long, as I keep one master list with themes within it) and identify the three items that I will do next. I order them 1, 2, 3 – then I execute them one by one. Once this is done, I might do this exercise again with three more, time permitting. As effective as this is for ticking things off the list, I find it most powerful in how much it calms me and enables me to focus on what can get done right now.

What's newly true? Change is the new black

To a person, Jacks and Jills told me what they know the most for certain is that they do not know what the future holds. They believe in their abilities to ride the waves of uncertainty by having the humility and grit to face it as it comes, coupled with the discipline of determining the right actions at the right times. Each time they would speak of decisive action, they would quickly add the inevitable reality they see that comes with such action: mistakes. Jacks and Jills express the importance of getting comfortable with the idea that we will make mistakes and we will need to look forward and fix them as they arise.

I fully understand that I have no idea what is coming down the road. None of us did and none of us still do. Even as we got into it, no one could predict what would happen, and no one can predict it now. But we know how to navigate as we go, and that's what I will continue to do.

Marc Lapides, President of Digital Marketing Partners

And for those who had more experience with rapid or intense change prior to the pandemic, they were able to find their footing a bit sooner, as they had the advantage of recognizing what was in front of them and knowing they had done similar before. "Change is the only constant" was merely conceptual to so many of us, yet today we all feel this firsthand. For our Jacks and Jills, they see the constancy of change and do what they can to help themselves and others understand how to navigate within these changing tides.

For me personally, I had the advantage of being a military brat. This means I have dealt with change in big ways all my life. Every two to three years I had a new city, new school, new friends...all of it. Even in my adult life I have kept up this pace. So my ability to not freak out in change and to look for the good in what comes next is something I rely on. It means not relying on the outside world to ground me. I try to help others see that it is the ability to ride the wave that gets you through, not fighting the current. Asking yourself, what do I need right now? And if you are not sure, get up and start walking and try to figure it out.

Lara Richardson, Chief Marketing Officer, Crown Media Family Networks

In the early stages of COVID, it turned to almost chaos in the sense of urgency of everything and in how much was changing. I thought, this sense of urgency is good as long as we don't let it turn into chaos...and this is true in my own life too. I don't just wait for things to happen, I make things happen. This has enhanced what I used to regard as a negative. I embrace the urgency where I used to look at it as a negative. We are all tenuous in our personal life. I weigh things each day and adjust. And I also work more on not putting things off. I get up in the morning and "eat the frog" (Mark Twain) and I feel so much better. I have encouraged my staff to not fear the urgency and the change, but to embrace it.

Jan Slater, Chief Marketing Officer at Gies College of Business, University of Illinois

Part of how I deal with the rapid change is really focusing on leaning into strengths—mine, and those around me. I learned a long time ago the importance of doing this, not fighting the dynamics nor trying to change people or organizations. This became so much more true in the pandemic and as we are emerging as well. So, when we think about the changes with remote work and in person and hybrid, rather than looking at it one way, look at what are the strength of being together and strengths of being apart—and how do we maximize both, versus fighting it?

**Pat Lafferty, Chief Operations Officer,
Acceleration Community of Companies**

CHAPTER TEN

Now What?
It's All in Your Head

Perhaps you have heard or read the famous parable (author unknown) called the Stallion Story, which tells us about a farmer who owns a stallion that he lovingly cares for. He also lives on the farm with his son. The farmer enters his stallion into the annual country fair competition. When his stallion wins first prize, the farmer's neighbors gather to congratulate him, to which the farmer only says calmly, *"Who knows what is good and what is bad?"* The neighbors are, of course, puzzled by his words.

The next week, some thieves who heard about the stallion's increased value come and steal the horse. When the neighbors commiserate with the farmer, they find him again very calm and again he says, *"Who knows what is good and what is bad?"*

Several days later, the spirited stallion escapes from the thieves and finds his way back to the farm, bringing with him a few wild mares he has befriended along the way. To his neighbors' excited rounds of congratulations, the old farmer once again says, *"Who knows what is good and what is bad?"*

A few weeks later, the farmer's son is thrown off one of the new mares as he is trying to break it in, and his leg is fractured. As the neighbors gather to commiserate with the old farmer, he once again reminds them, *"Who knows what is good and what is bad?"*

The following week, the imperial army marches through the village, drafting all eligible young men for the war that has just broken out. The old farmer's son is spared due to his fractured leg. The neighbors no longer bother to come to the old farmer to congratulate him. By now they know what his response will be: *"Who knows what is good and what is bad?"*

While this is a dramatic example that I cannot directly relate to, since I don't own a horse, I have not lived in a small village and thankfully have never faced any of my children going off to war, this author's message is the most relevant I have found to the world we live in today: when we face seemingly difficult experiences, we really don't know what they mean at the time, and only with time will we know what helps or hinders us. Said another way, all of our experiences are determined by how we regard them, not by the experiences themselves.

I will take this a big step further, borrowing from Shirzad Chamine's *Positive Intelligence* premise that in every situation, especially those that seem difficult, there is a gift...you just have to look for it. This does not mean that we are happy that difficult things happen, rather that we develop the habit of looking for the good, even in—and especially in—what feel like difficult experiences.

Example: a small business owner of a live events-based company lost 70 percent of her revenue with the cancellation of live events during the pandemic. As she managed the fallout and considered shuttering the business, she decided to invest in technology that more effectively manages the logistics and production needed for hybrid (live and virtual) events. Once the shutdown restrictions lessened enough to bring some people on site, she found herself with a superior tool that no competitor had, and plans to triple her revenue this year.

Example: a Jill in charge of a large marketing department in a financial services organization lost two thirds of her staff and her budget in the shutdown, and decided to leave the company that no longer needed such a senior leader. After months of unemployment and forced time at home, she began looking at smaller organizations and landed a position with a start-up where she feels she has found her calling and her people—the best culture she has ever experienced.

Example: a Jill who had chosen to leave her senior marketing positioning a few months before the shutdown found herself unemployed for over a year due to the dynamics of the pandemic. At first resisting but then embracing this additional time to reflect and conduct a thoughtful search, she landed a position with a mission-based organization that combines her personal passions with her professional ones.

And I could go on. While not every "bad turn" leads to an obvious gift, the gifts are there if you look. The gifts may not feel like they "outweigh" the difficulties, but remember that this "weight" is in your perception, and therefore your power, to flip the script if you want to and apply effort to do so.

An important exception to this outlook of difficult experiences providing gifts is grief and loss. While gifts can be found in any situation, I do not want to underestimate the pain of these kinds of experiences, especially when they are of a tragic nature. Nonetheless, I have seen and suspect you may have as well, individuals who have faced great suffering and seem to find the joy of life in spite of, or perhaps because of, the suffering. One famous example is Peter Barton, co-author of *Not Fade Away*, a memoir of his life as he was diagnosed with cancer and died at age 51. Peter was the founder and CEO of Liberty Media, and was an advocate for innovative programming of his time such as Discovery Channel, Black Entertainment Television and QVC. Peter states, "the gift" in this way, *"My disease has been good for me in a certain sense. It has made me more accepting, gentler. Earlier in my life I might have been ashamed of this, seen it as a sign of weakness. Now I'm proud of it. I'm growing unafraid."*

He also shared, *"Once my unproductive anger about this lousy break started to subside, I began thinking less about what cancer was doing to me and more about what it was doing for me. And I realized something sort of wonderful. Cancer was giving me the opportunity to live more attentively, more wholly in the moment."*

The truth is, it *is* all in our heads: how we perceive our lives, how we regard our relationships, how we look at our level of success or lack of, how happy we define ourselves as being. In fact, most especially how happy we regard ourselves. Mental health challenges are real and we must not underestimate them, yet our ability to shift and shape our own minds when we set out to do so is the strongest tool we have. What we believe, we are. What we are, we believe. I personally have been practicing mantras, affirmations, deep breathing, meditation, journaling…and I tell you this stuff really works.

I cannot linger on this subject without citing Viktor Frankl, author of *Man's Search for Meaning* after his experience as in concentration camps watching his mother, father and wife perish. Frankl learned through intense suffering and by observing the suffering of others, that suffering was a state of mind, and therefore optional: *"Everything can be taken from a man but one thing: the last of the human freedoms—to choose one's attitude in any given set of circumstances, to choose one's own way."* And *"Forces beyond your control can take away everything you possess except one thing, your freedom to choose how you will respond to the situation."*

If you find this intriguing and you are curious to see what

kind of a shift you can make yourself, *Man's Search for Meaning* by Viktor Frankl and *The Obstacle Is the Way* by Ryan Holiday are excellent sources for understanding and reimagining our life's experiences. For practical tools and guidance that you can build into a daily practice, I recommend *Miracle Mornings* or *Positive Intelligence*. *Positive Intelligence* teaches a different relationship with the voices in our head who are often negative or trigger negativity. *Miracle Mornings* provides an early morning routine that can displace our carrying our perceived burdens of the day before, the week before, the year before. *Miracle Mornings* offers tools to reframe the new day and bring a renewed perspective, even when or perhaps especially when, we feel tired and overwhelmed.

What does any of this have to do with marketing?

That, my friends, is one of the greatest gifts I have gained from writing these new chapters. Connecting and reconnecting with the Jacks and Jills that I admire and am inspired by gave me a whole new perspective this time around. We talked about marketing, yes, but we spoke the most about our humanity, our vulnerability, our growth and our learning. This is the backbone of what the best marketers understand, and it is the backbone of what makes life, life. Perhaps this enhanced perspective makes the *most* sense that it would come from marketers, whose life's work is to deeply understand people and who never look at failure as failure, but only as learning. And when we understand that life is about learning, about connecting with one another and about living the values that truly express who we are, we come to see that we can be more than our circumstances and achieve more than we thought possible. Yes, we get tired. We get frustrated. We get discouraged. We get scared. This is to be expected and, for a short time, should be honored. But when we fall down the hill, we don't stay down. We get up, we dust off, we scale again.

EPILOGUE

By Ann Mukherjee
(former) Global Chief Marketing Officer, SC Johnson
(now) Chairman and CEO, Pernod Ricard NA

I have been a marketer for over 25 years. I have dedicated my craft to making marketing the fuel for sustainable growth – by perfecting the science of predictable human behavior and turning it into the art of persuasion and purchase for the brands that drive profitable share growth. It was this track record that got me appointed as Chairman and CEO of Pernod Ricard North America in December of 2019. I entered my role with a proven track record of accelerating growth and a commercial playbook that brought the forces of demand and supply uniquely together to drive advantaged growth for a company. This was something Pernod Ricard was looking for as the #2 global spirits and wine company. They hired me to jumpstart the business on their quest to be #1 in the world.

Little did I or Pernod Ricard know that three months later, that proven playbook that I had perfected would be massively challenged as the world plunged into a global pandemic. Overnight, I was faced with not only how to navigate a business that was facing uncertainty and turmoil, but an organization that needed to be kept safe not just from COVID, but from a parallel epidemic of political, social and racial upheavals.

In this book, Nancie talks about the power of Positive Intelligence and in the midst of suffering and pain, finding the gifts of possibilities and learning to transform and elevate. It is in this belief system of Positive Intelligence that we found our next S curve of growth to catapult the Pernod Ricard North American business to its highest performance in the company's history.

Hindsight is always 20/20. Given what I know today, I think I would have done just fine as a first time CEO at Pernod Ricard had the pandemic not happened. It would have been another chapter in my book of driving high performance leadership. Instead, the pandemic gave me the gift to write a new book, not about a continuing saga of performance, but one of that was about Advancing Through Ambiguity.

The pandemic forced me to face my vulnerabilities, to re-evaluate what it means to be a CEO. And rather than looking at other CEO's, who were probably as shaken as I was, I went back to my CMO skills and training. I became curious again, I began to learn anew, observe and listen so I could better define the new problems to solve in this *now* normal of VUCA. Quickly I discovered that advancing through ambiguity meant that we need to distill all possible courses of issues and actions into those that mattered and intersect that with what was in our control. This gave us focus and purpose to drive action, experimentation, continuous learning and deliver desired outcomes.

For me, Nancie has always played the role of Sherpa. Her thoughtful, reflective, inventive skills have therapeutic power for people looking to push beyond the expected and thrive despite challenges. These latest chapters help to reframe what we know, to help us not only be better but transform what we do so we can surf the future vs drowning in its uncertainty. She helped me reframe the 3 C's of customer, culture and creativity.

Customers are the lifeblood of any prosperous business, but in my new role I widened my view to include employees as my customers. Now more than ever, it isn't just consumers who want to buy into your brands, but employees who want to buy into the company they choose to work for. Understanding their needs, I would argue is as important, if not more, than that of your consumers. Without committed employees you won't have anyone to win over your consumers and customers.

In this new world of agile working, fostering proven company cultures that are the lifeblood and the secret sauce of success is very challenging. The art is not changing the what of your culture, but instead challenging the how you give it life. This takes new beliefs and behaviors that challenges norms and established practices.

Finally, the most powerful lesson I learned was about creativity. Creativity is not just about the magic of marketing. Instead, creativity is the oxygen to business growth. It can be applied to how we overcome supply disruptions, talent wars, raw material shortages, go to market obstacles, environmental issues and societal impacts. Creativity is about helping others to see new possibilities through the power of ideas and storytelling. It's about getting people to re-define problems and see things in new ways.

Nancie's explorations across these many dimensions are thought provoking. She does it with warmth, humility and thoughtfulness. The true gift of her book is to help you, the reader, find your unique power so you can leverage it to make the positive change and impact you desire.

It's now time for you to go. Go unleash your gifts - not just to make what is possible, possible - but to turn what you may think is impossible into something that is possible. Nancie has certainly done that for me, and it has given me my next S curve of growth. Now it's your turn!

ACKNOWLEDGEMENTS

This book was a labor of love that took a village to birth. I must first acknowledge that it could not have happened without the tireless help of my team at Noetic. I am deeply grateful for their passion, interest and hours spent and continuously inspired by their insights and collaboration.

Thank you to my gifted editor, Alyson Gold Weinberg, without whose help this book would still sit as a draft trapped in my computer. Every time I got stuck, she unstuck me with fresh ideas, a warm smile and infectious enthusiasm for what we were building together. Thank you to Emily Schwartz, my new editor, who helped piece together the updated chapters.

I want to acknowledge all of the marketing Jacks and Jills I interviewed, who truly made the book what it is: an insightful portrayal of what it takes to scale the heights today, in their own words. They were exceedingly generous with their time and their candid responses.

Thank you to my dear friend and amazing leader, Ann Mukherjee, who did me the honor of writing the both the original and updated Forward for the book, as well as emotionally supporting me through the journey of this book creation.

I want to thank my dear friends Kristen Wheeden and Karen Irwin who generously opened their homes to me when life was especially chaotic and I needed a quiet space to write.

I must acknowledge my skilled copyeditor and proofreader, Mary Beth Conlee and Madonna Aldrich. And gifted designer, Jenn Spencer, who during so many late-night meetings to get the book designed, always delivered with a smile and an amazing design eye. And did so again with the new edition.

I want to thank the amazing women of WPO, who supported and cheered me on; my book advisors, who had authored already and helped me understand the hard lessons they had learned so that I could benefit from them: Jeff Rum, Jim Schecksler, Ivana Taylor, Tom Tobin, Steve Lance and Rocky Romanella. I want to thank EOS and Randy Taussig for helping us learn how to set rocks and a quarterly cadence that enabled the structure that helped bring the book to fruition.

I want to acknowledge my oldest daughter, Sydney Jane, who ran the last miles of the marathon with me and believed in me more than I ever could believe in myself.

Now having completed the new edition, I want to add my thanks to the new and "repeat" village that helped me bring this to fruition: I want to thank the Jacks and Jills who took the time to speak with me – some for a second time from the first edition – and to share their thoughts courageously and candidly. And again, I must thank my amazing Noetic team who helped me emotionally, logistically and insightfully at every step along the path.

For all these angels in my life and what they have given to me and this body of work, I am amazingly blessed and my gratitude is more than I can put into words.

WORKS CITED

Smith, E.E. "Are You Left- or Right-Brain Dominant?" *Psychology Today*, Sussex Publishers, www.psychologytoday.com/blog/not-born-yesterday/201210/are-you-left-or-right-brain-dominant.

Bacon, Jeremie. "The Difference in Being Customer-Centric vs. Customer-Focused." *Journeys*, journeys.getsynap.com/the-difference-in-being-customer-centric-vs.-customer-focused.

Brooks, David. "Putting Grit in Its Place." *The New York Times*, The New York Times, 10 May 2016, www.nytimes.com/2016/05/10/opinion/putting-grit-in-its-place.html.

Brown, Tim. "Transcript of 'Tales of Creativity and Play.'" *TED: Ideas Worth Spreading*, www.ted.com/talks/tim_brown_on_creativity_and_play/transcript.

Cabane, Olivia Fox. *The Charisma Myth: Master the Art of Personal Magnetism*. Portfolio Penguin, 2013.

Dethmer, Jim, et al. *The 15 Commitments of Conscious Leadership: a New Paradigm for Sustainable Success*. Conscious Leadership Group, 2015.

Duckworth, Angela. *Grit: The Power of Passion and Perseverance*. New York: Scribner, 2016.

Dweck, Carol. "What Having a 'Growth Mindset' Actually Means." *Harvard Business Review*, 13 Jan. 2016, hbr.org/2016/01/what-having-a-growth-mindset-actually-means.

Economy, Peter. "Top 10 Skills Every Great Leader Needs to Succeed." *Inc.com*, Inc., 30 Dec. 2014, www.inc.com/peter-economy/top-10-skills-every-great-leader-needs-to-succeed.html.

Edelman, David C. "Four Ways to Get More Value from Digital Marketing." *McKinsey & Company*, www.mckinsey.com/business-functions/marketing-and-sales/our-insights/four-ways-to-get-more-value-from-digital-marketing.

Featherstone, Dave. "Why Art And Science Are More Closely Related Than You Think." *Forbes*, Forbes Magazine, 16 Mar. 2016, www.forbes.com/sites/quora/2016/03/16/why-art-and-science-are-more-closely-related-than-you-think/.

Gensler, M. Arthur and Michael Lindenmayer. *Art's Principles: 50 Years of Hard-Learned Lessons in Building a World-Class Professional Services Firm*. Wilson Lafferty, 2015.

Gladwell, Malcolm. *The Tipping Point: How Little Things Can Make a Big Difference*. Boston: Little, Brown and Company, 2000.

Goleman, Daniel, et al. "What Makes a Leader?" *Harvard Business Review*, 18 July 2017, hbr.org/2004/01/what-makes-a-leader.

"How Uber Uses Data to Improve Their Service and Create the New Wave of Mobility." *A Deep Dive Into Facebook Advertising - Learn How To Make It Work For Your Business!*, blog.kissmetrics.com/how-uber-uses-data/.

Jeffers, Susan J. *Feel the Fear and Do It Anyway*. Vermilion, 2013.

Kerpen, Carrie. *Work It: Secrets for Success from the Boldest Women in Business*. A TarcherPerigee Book, 2018.

Lencioni, Patrick. *The Five Dysfunctions of a Team: a Workshop for Team Leaders*. Pfeiffer, 2012.

Lombrozo, Tania. "The Truth About The Left Brain / Right Brain Relationship." *NPR*, NPR, 2 Dec. 2013, www.npr.org/sections/13.7/2013/12/02/248089436/the-truth-about-the-left-brain-right-brain-relationship.

Maeda, John. 11 July, 2013, *Artists and Scientists: More Alike Than Different*. https://blogs.scientificamerican.com/guest-blog/artists-and-scientists-more-alike-than-different/.

McClain, Mark. "How Corporate Culture Can Make (Or Break)
Your Organization." *Forbes*, Forbes Magazine, 6 Nov. 2017,
www.forbes.com/sites/forbestechcouncil/2017/11/06/how-
corporate-culture-can-make-or-break-your-organization/.

Moser-Wellman, Annette. *The Five Faces of Genius: the
Skills to Master Ideas at Work*. Viking, 2001.

Olson, Max. "Generalists vs. Specialists (And the Specialist's
Dilemma)." *FutureBlind*, 31 July 2015, futureblind.com/2011/07/29/
generalists-vs-specialists-and-the-specialists-dilemma/.

Pearson, David. "Exploding the Myth of the Scientific vs Artistic Mind."
The Conversation, The Conversation, 21 June 2018, theconversation.
com/exploding-the-myth-of-the-scientific-vs-artistic-mind-57843.

Pereira, Steven Wolfe. "Are You Building a 21st Century
Brand?" *Ad Age*, 5 Mar. 2018, adage.com/article/
quantcast/building-a-21st-century-brand/312554/.

Porter, Michael E. "What Is Strategy?" *Harvard Business
Review*, 3 Oct. 2017, hbr.org/1996/11/what-is-strategy.

Rothenberg, Randall. "How Brands Grow in Crisis."
How to Be a 21st Century Brand. IAB Annual Leadership
Meeting, 12 Feb. 2018, Palm Desert, California.

Ryan, Liz. 10 January, 2015, *Why 'Jack Of All Trades' Is The Worst
Personal Brand*. https://www.forbes.com/sites/lizryan/2015/01/20/
why-jack-of-all-trades-is-the-worst-personal-brand/#7dd2b24a2438

Silva, Jason. "Art and Science Are Two Sides of the Same Coin."
Big Think, Big Think, 24 Aug. 2013, bigthink.com/in-their-own-
words/art-and-science-are-two-sides-of-the-same-coin.

Slyke, Michelle Van. "4 Ways to Know Your Customer
Better." *Inc.com*, Inc., 22 Jan. 2018, www.inc.com/michelle-
van-slyke/4-ways-to-know-your-customer-better.html.

Spyer, Simon. "3 Key Performance Indicators Every
CMO Should Focus On." *How to Prioritise Your Strategic
Marketing Objectives*, www.conduithub.com/blog/3-key-
performance-indicators-every-cmo-should-focus-on.

Stafford, Tom. "Future - Why Are We so Curious?" *BBC News*, BBC, 19 June 2012, www.bbc.com/future/story/20120618-why-are-we-so-curious.

Svoboda, Elizabeth. "Cultivating Curiosity." *Psychology Today*, Sussex Publishers, 2006, www.psychologytoday. com/articles/200609/cultivating-curiosity.

Valchev, Marin and Unni. "Analytical Skills Examples | How To Improve Them: Guide." *Business Skills & Software*, 6 June 2017, www.businessphrases.net/analytical-skills/.

Venkatraman, Rohini. "You're 96 Percent Less Creative Than You Were as a Child. Here's How to Reverse That." *Inc. com*, Inc., 18 Jan. 2018, www.inc.com/rohini-venkatraman/4-ways-to-get-back-creativity-you-had-as-a-kid.html.

Wickman, Gino. *Traction: Get a Grip on Your Business*. BenBella Books, 2011.

Blum, Kelly. "Path to Recovery: The Annual CMO Spend Survey 2020." *Business Wire*, 1 July 2020, www.businesswire. com/news/home/20200701005139/en/Gartner-Says-CMOs-Remain-Optimistic-About-Budgets-Post-COVID19-Despite-Bleak-Outlook-from-C-Suite-Colleagues.

Briedis, Holly, et al. "Adapting to the next normal in retail: The customer experience imperative." *McKinsey*, 14 May 2020, www. mckinsey.com/industries/retail/our-insights/adapting-to-the-next-normal-in-retail-the-customer-experience-imperative.

Carufel, Richard. "The Global COVID-19 Effect on Market Research Data Collection." *Agility PR Solutions*, 19 October 2020, www.agilitypr.com/pr-news/public-relations/as-budgets-get-cut-market-research-nose-dives-during-covid/.

Chamine, Shirzad. *Positive Intelligence*. Greenleaf Book Group Press, 2012.

Clark, Marsha. *Embracing Your Power: A Woman's Path to Authentic Leadership and Meaningful Relationships*. Greenleaf Book Group Press, 2022.

"Creativity Booms as Americans Adapt to Life During the Pandemic – Canva Study Reveals." *PR Newswire*, 3 December 2020, www.prnewswire.com/news-releases/creativity-booms-as-americans-adapt-to-life-during-the-pandemic--canva-study-reveals-301185479.

Elrod, Hal. *The Miracle Morning: The Not-so-obvious Secret Guaranteed to Transform Your Life Before 8 AM. Journal.* Hal Elrod International, 2013.

Frankl, Viktor E. *Man's Search for Meaning.* Translated by William J. Winslade, et al., Beacon Press, 2006.

Holiday, Ryan. *The Obstacle Is the Way: The Timeless Art of Turning Trials Into Triumph.* Penguin Publishing Group, 2014.

Holtom, Brooks, et al. "5 Tips for Communicating with Employees During a Crisis." *Harvard Business Review,* 9 July 2020, hbr.org/2020/07/5-tips-for-communicating-with-employees-during-a-crisis.

Medina, Elizabeth. "Job Satisfaction and Employee Turnover Intention: What does Organizational Culture Have To Do With It?" *Columbia Academic Commons*, 1 February 2013, academiccommons.columbia.edu/doi/10.7916/D8DV1S08.

Schwartz, Tony. "Escalating Demands at Work Hurt Employees and Companies (Published 2015)." *The New York Times*, 5 June 2015, www.nytimes.com/2015/06/06/business/dealbook/excessive-demands-at-work-create-a-humanitarian-crisis.html.

Shames, Laurence, and Peter Barton. *Not Fade Away: A Short Life Well Lived.* HarperCollins, 2004.

Siu, Eric. "It Really Pays to Have a Rich Company Culture [Infographic]." *Entrepreneur,* www.entrepreneur.com/article/238640.

Tatum, Megan. "What skills will marketers need to face the post-pandemic world?" *Marketing Week*, 19 January 2021, www.marketingweek.com/marketers-skills-post-pandemic/.

Vailshery, Lionel Sujay. "Zoom daily meeting participants worldwide 2020." *Statista*, www.statista.com/statistics/1253972/zoom-daily-meeting-participants-global/.